A Williamson  Book

At the Zoo!

Explore the Animal World   with Craft Fun

by Judy Press

Illustrations by Jenny Campbell

WILLIAMSON PUBLISHING • CHARLOTTE, VERMONT

Library of Congress Cataloging-in-Publication Data

Press, Judy, 1944–
    At the zoo! : explore the animal world with craft fun / by Judy Press.
        p. cm. — (A little hands book)
    Includes index.
    Summary: Provides instructions for creating all kinds of animals found in zoos along with information about these creatures.
    ISBN 1-885593-61-9 (pbk.)
    1. Handicraft—Juvenile literature. 2. Animals in art—Juvenile literature. [1. Animals in art. 2. Handicraft. 3. Zoo animals.] I. Title. II. Series.

TT160 .P77796 2002
745.5—dc21

2002026821

Little Hands® series editor: **Susan Williamson**
Project editor: **Dana Pierson**
Interior design: **Julia Reich**
Illustrations: **Jenny Campbell**
Cover design: **Monkey Barrel Design**
Cover photography: animals—**Peter Coleman** • children—**David A. Seaver**
Printing: **Capital City Press**

Williamson Publishing Co.
P.O. Box 185
Charlotte, VT 05445
(800) 234-8791

Manufactured in the United States of America

10 9 8 7 6 5 4 3 2 1

Little Hands®, *Kids Can!*®, *Tales Alive!*®, and *Kaleidoscope Kids*® are registered trademarks of Williamson Publishing.

Good Times™, *Little Hands Story Corner*™, and *Quick Starts for Kids!*™ are trademarks of Williamson Publishing.

Dedication

To my father, Morris Abraham, with love.

Acknowledgments

I wish to thank the following people for their support and encouragement in the writing of this book: My husband, Allan, and my children; The Mt. Lebanon Public Library; the Carnegie Library of Pittsburgh; Carol Baicker McKee; and Andrea Perry. I would also like to thank Page. She may not roar like a lion, but she's our favorite little cat.

This book would not have been possible without the talent and dedication of the following people at Williamson Publishing: Susan and Jack Williamson, Dana Pierson, Emily Stetson, June Roelle, Vicky Congdon, Jean Silveira, Merietta McKenzie, and Julie Farrington. A special thanks to designer Julia Reich and illustrator Jenny Campbell for their creative talents.

Contents

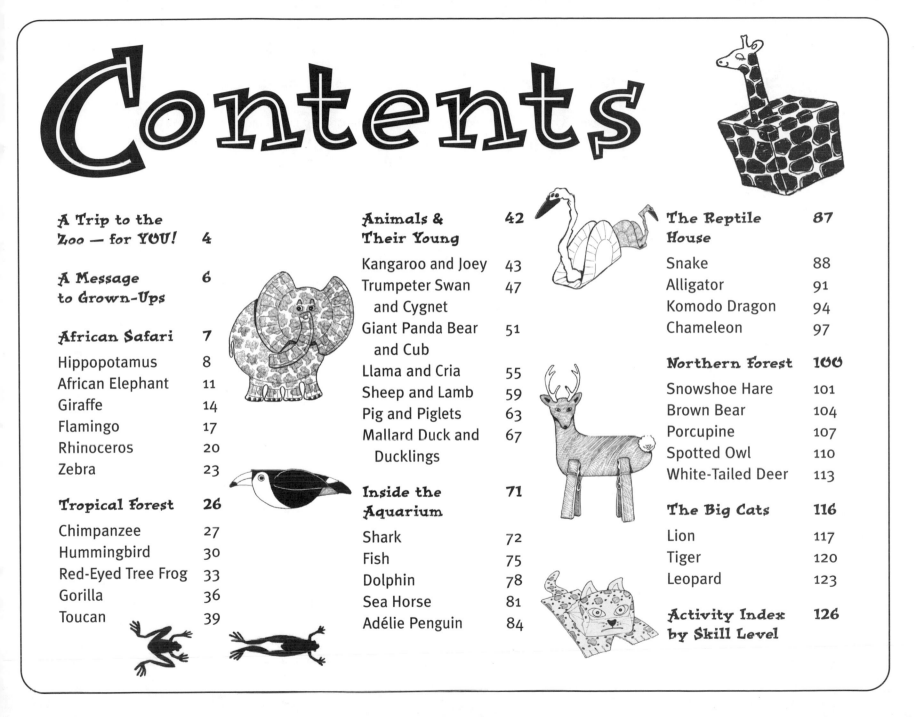

A Trip to the Zoo — for YOU!

The lion isn't in the jungle.
The turtle isn't in the sea.
The chipmunk isn't in the forest.
Where do you think they could be?

At the mall? In the bathtub? At the zoo?

At the Zoo!

We're off to the zoo! When we arrive, we can barely believe all of the animals we find there! Why it's almost as if parts of the whole world are here, for each animal's home has been re-created here so the animals will be very comfortable.

It's very important for animals at the zoo to feel comfortable in their zoo homes. A *zoo architect* designs homes, or *habitats* (places to live), to be as close to the animals' natural habitats as possible. This means that you get to watch them play and sleep just as they might do out in the wild.

4

At the zoo, you can see many animals—everything from anteaters to zebras. Some of the animals were born at the zoo, but most came from faraway places.

Lots of people at the zoo take care of the animals you see there. Zookeepers work hard to make sure that every animal is healthy, comfortable, well fed, and active. If an animal gets sick or injured, the *veterinarian*, or animal doctor, takes care of it at the veterinary hospital. This is a very busy place, where most of the zoo's animals get regular checkups (just like your dog or cat does).

Much of the food for zoo animals comes from a *commissary*, which looks like a big kitchen. Every morning people thaw frozen meat, cook vegetables, and weigh fresh fruits and vegetables that are put into plastic tubs. The tubs are then delivered to animals all over the zoo. (Many animals need to eat their vegetables just like people do!)

Some *species*, or kinds, of animals cannot be seen at any zoo because they are *extinct*. This means that there are no longer any living members of that species anywhere in the world. Many animals are becoming extinct because people are destroying the forests and grasslands where the animals live. If you see our "endangered" stamp with an animal that you meet, you will know that the animal is in danger of becoming extinct.

And remember, when you visit a zoo, not only are you watching the animals, the animals are watching you, too!

A Message to Grown-Ups

Today, zoos are multifaceted enterprises encompassing animal research and breeding, educational programs, and the daily care of hundreds of remarkable animals and plants. Zoo animals are well fed and do not face the dangers they must overcome in nature. Once a symbol of our ability to capture and confine wild animals, zoos today are links with the natural world that reflect our intention to sustain all varieties of life.

Zoos have changed because the habitats around the world are in trouble. Wild, unspoiled lands are disappearing at an alarming rate, encroached upon and exploited by human development. With the loss of their habitats, animals are also disappearing. As the human population grows, the wild areas of the globe diminish, and many animals may become extinct before scientists even have a chance to identify them. Zoos help to keep species from dying out. Whenever a rare animal baby is born in captivity, it's a step toward saving a species from extinction.

Animal Art & Crafts

Specific instructions are provided for each project, but always allow children to make choices and follow their muses. Avoid holding up as examples perfectly completed projects that will intimidate and stifle creativity. Encourage new ideas, fanciful designs, and individualized interpretations so that each piece of art reflects the creativity and mood of the child who made it.

A number of the animals in this book are made with small cardboard cereal boxes and tissue boxes. This is a perfect size for chidren to "pretend play" with their creations. Any size cardboard box can be used, however. Use a cardboard carton to create animals like the ones shown in the center of the cover. Large versions lend themselves quite well to a birthday party activity or group effort, but keep in mind when working with large cartons that adult help is mandatory, especially with the utility knife needed to cut through thick cardboard. It's a good idea for the adult to precut the head and neck for the children to decorate.

Some projects in the book are more complicated than others (see *Activity Index by Skill Level*, page 126). There are symbols next to each project: One pair of scissors means that the craft is uncomplicated, two mean that more time is needed, and three mean that the craft is challenging and requires the assistance of an adult.

Always remember to work in a well-ventilated room, assess your young crafters' propensity to put small objects in their mouths (choose and control access to materials accordingly), and work with nontoxic materials. Remember that younger siblings may pick up odds and ends from the floor or pull items off the table's edge. When scissors are used by children, please use child safety scissors, never sharp adult scissors.

African Safari

Do you know what a *safari* is? It's a special trip that people take to Africa so they can see all the wonderful wildlife in many kinds of animal habitats. Africa has rain forests and deserts, and it also has wide-open spaces, called *savannas*, which are like seas of grass dotted with the occasional bush and tree. They provide a varied food supply for many animals.

At the zoo, grassland habitats are built so that you feel as if you're on safari, so you may or may not see the animals there, especially if they're sleeping by a log or hiding in the bushes! Another thing you may notice about grassland habitats in the zoo is that they are surrounded by water. This is so animals will be safe from people getting too close, and people will be safe from the animals, too!

I'm big and fat and
round and gray.
The river is where
I like to stay.

ENDANGERED

Site: south of the Sahara
Desert, and the lakes, rivers,
and swamps of eastern
and central Africa

Am I a hippopotamus? An alligator? A peacock?

What you need:

- Knife (for grown-up use only)
- Large raw potato
- Raw carrot
- White and black tempera paints
- Light-colored construction paper
- Paintbrush
- Black marker

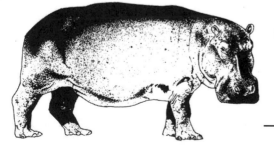

Hippopotamus

What you do:

1. Ask a grown-up to cut the potato in half the long way and to cut the carrot so that it has a round, flat end.

2. Mix white paint with a drop of black paint in a dish or lid to make gray. To make the hippo's body, dip the flat side of the potato into the paint; press onto the light-colored paper.

3. To make the hippo's head, dip the flat end of the carrot into the paint; press it onto one end of the potato print three times.

4. Use the brush to paint the hippo's legs and tail. Let dry.

5. Use the marker to draw the hippo's eyes, nose, ears, toes, and wrinkles.

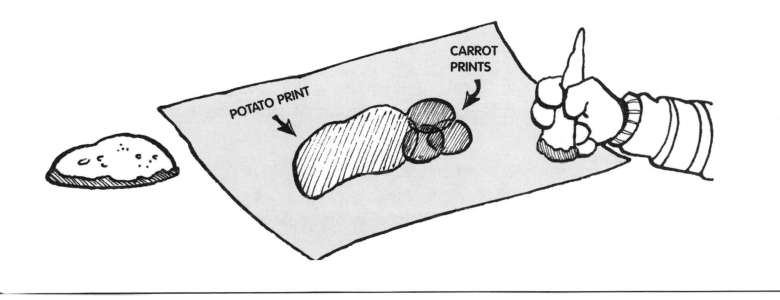

POTATO PRINT

CARROT PRINTS

Little Hands Story Corner™

See if your local video store has *Fantasia*. Can you spot the dancing hippos? Or, to learn more about the hippo and its African friends, read *When Hippo Was Hairy and Other Tales from Africa* by Nick Greaves.

Ask the Zookeeper

Q: How much does a baby hippo weigh?

A: When they're born, hippos already weigh 50 to 90 pounds (22.5 to 40.5 kg). Wow! Do you weigh as much as a newborn hippo yet?

Getting to Know Us

Hippo tantrums. When hippos get angry, hungry, or uncomfortable, they open their mouths wide to let out deep roars and growls. What do you do when you're angry or uncomfortable?

A leg to stand on. See how short and fat hippo legs are? That's so they can hold the heavy weight of a hippo. Compare hippo legs to the legs of a flamingo (page 17). How are they different? Could a flamingo's legs hold up a hippo? Draw a picture of a hippo on flamingo legs.

I carry a trunk,
but I'm not going away.
My skin is all wrinkled,
my color is gray.

Am I a lamb? An alligator? An elephant?

What you need:

- Child safety scissors
- 2 white paper plates (1 large, 1 small)
- White and black tempera paints
- Sponge
- Paper fastener*
- Black marker
- Glue stick (optional)
- Wiggly eyes (optional)

* Note: Children may put small objects in their mouths. An adult should control the supply of paper fasteners and distribute them as needed.

African Elephant

What you do:

1. Cut around the sides of the large paper plate for the elephant's body. Cut into the side of the plate for a tail. Cut into the bottom of the plate for legs and feet.

2. Cut around the small plate for the elephant's head and ears. Use a scrap of the ridged edge for the trunk.

3. Mix white paint with a drop of black paint in a dish or lid to make gray. Dab the sponge into the gray paint and press lightly onto the elephant. Let dry.

4. Ask a grown-up to use a paper fastener to attach the elephant's head and trunk to the body. Use the marker to draw the elephant's eyes (or glue on wiggly eyes) and toes.

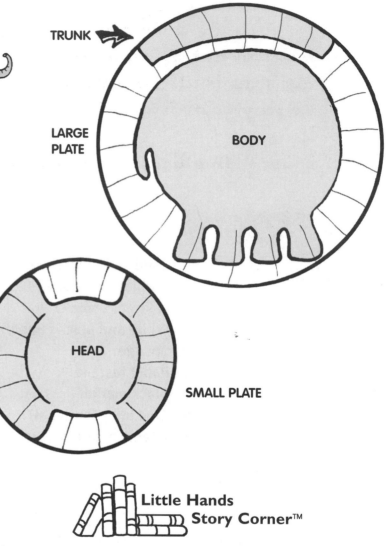

TRUNK

LARGE PLATE

BODY

HEAD

SMALL PLATE

Little Hands Story Corner™

Read the classic *The Story of Babar, the Little Elephant* by Jean de Brunhoff.

Have trunk, will travel. Elephants use their trunks for smelling, feeling, breathing, sucking up water, grasping food, and making loud trumpeting calls. Try holding a paper-towel tube over your nose for a pretend trunk; then, make loud elephant calls while you walk around swinging your trunk from side to side.

Say what? Elephants can "talk" to each other over great distances. They use sounds that humans cannot hear. In addition to talking, what ways do you use to tell people what you want them to know? Do you make faces to show your feelings?

Ask the Zookeeper

Q: Why do elephants have such big ears?

A: What's your best guess? I thought that it might be to swat flies, but actually elephants flap their ears to cool themselves down. It's like having built-in air-conditioning! What do you do to cool down? Perhaps you take a shower or run under the sprinkler. Elephants do something like that, too. They spray themselves with water that they suck up into their trunks!

My neck is long,
my spots are brown.
I can look up,
but it's hard to bend down!

Am I a walrus? A giraffe?
A horse?

What you need:

- Tall cardboard tissue box
- Tape
- Scraps of cereal-box cardboard
- Scissors (for grown-up use only)
- Child safety scissors
- Brown and black markers
- Scrap of brown construction paper

Giraffe

What you do:

1. Open up the tissue box so it lies flat. Re-form the box so it is inside out. Tape to hold. Tape a scrap of cardboard over the hole in the box. Ask a grown-up to cut a slit in one side of the box.

ASK AN ADULT
TO CUT HERE

2. Cut out the neck and head of the giraffe from the scrap cardboard.

Use the brown marker to draw the giraffe's spots. Use the black marker to draw the eyes, nose, and mouth.

3. Insert the giraffe's neck into the slit and tape to hold. Cut out the giraffe's tail from the scrap of brown paper and tape to the box.

Little Hands Story Corner™

Read *A Giraffe and a Half* by Shel Silverstein.

Ask the Zookeeper

Q: How do giraffes reach the food to eat on the ground?

A: They spread their legs, which lowers their shoulders so their heads can reach the ground. Can you touch the ground without bending your knees? If you spread your legs apart, is it easier to touch the ground?

Getting to Know Us

It's a stretch! Giraffes are so tall that they eat leaves from the tops of trees. Ask a grown-up to help you stand on a step stool. Do you see things differently now that you are taller? What things can you reach that you couldn't reach before?

Size it up. A giraffe's neck can be 6 feet (180 cm) long. Lay six pairs of grown-up shoes end to end to see how long that is. Lie down with your shoulders at the first pair. Imagine if your neck were that long. How would you bend down to pick up your toys?

Baby giraffe! To make a baby giraffe, follow the directions above using a ¾ oz (21 g) cereal box.

My body is long
and tall and pink.
I dip my head low
to take a drink.

Am I a duck? A sheep? A flamingo?

Site: The vivid red subspecies lives in the Caribbean, the Yucatan (Mexico), and the West Indies to the coast of northeastern South America. The paler pink subspecies lives throughout the Mediterranean and Africa, east to northwestern India.

What you need:

- Pencil
- Large white paper plate
- Child safety scissors
- White and red tempera paints
- White construction paper
- Sponge
- Black marker

Flamingo

What you do:

1. Draw a picture of a flamingo in the center of the paper plate.

Ask a grown-up to help you cut out the flamingo without cutting into the rim of the plate.

2. Add a drop of white paint to the red paint in a dish or lid to make pink. Hold the plate with the cut-out flamingo against the white paper. Dip the sponge into the paint and dab it over the stencil. Let dry.

3. Move the flamingo stencil to another place on the white paper, and paint over it. Let dry. Repeat one more time. Use the marker to draw feathers, beaks, and eyes on your flamingos.

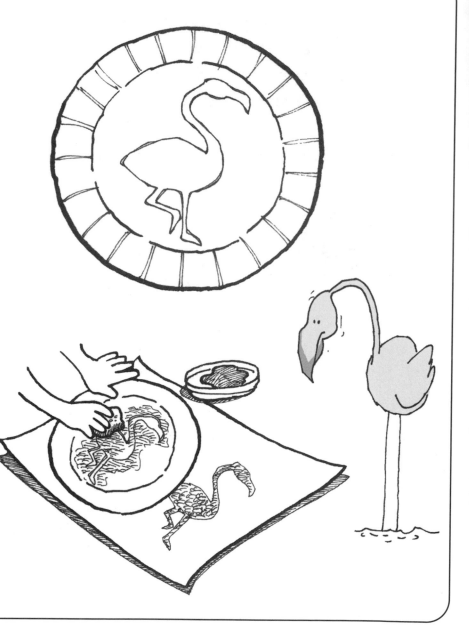

Ask the Zookeeper

Q: Why are flamingos pink?

A: Has anyone ever said to you, "You are what you eat"? Well, with flamingos, it's really true. Flamingos are pink because they eat shrimp and other things that have red color in them. The color goes straight into the flamingos' feathers as they grow! Do your hands turn color when you hold certain foods for a long time? Wouldn't it be funny if you turned purple when you drank grape juice, red when you gobbled strawberries, or bright green when you ate fresh string beans?

Getting to Know Us

Pretend play. Count the number of seconds you can stand on one leg like a flamingo. After some practice, play a game with your friends to see who can stand flamingo-style the longest.

I have a horn
that I cannot play.
A ton or two
is what I weigh.

Site: bushy plains and rugged hills, in isolated areas of central and southern Africa

ENDANGERED

Am I a fox? A rhinoceros? A deer?

What you need:

- Cereal box, ¾ oz (21 g)
- Tape
- Child safety scissors
- Scrap of gray construction paper
- Black marker

Rhinoceros

What you do:

1. Open the bottom and side panels of the cereal box so it lies flat. Re-form the box so it's inside out. Tape to hold, but leave the lid untaped.

2. Cut out the rhino's head and neck from the construction paper. Make the neck long enough to fold a tab.

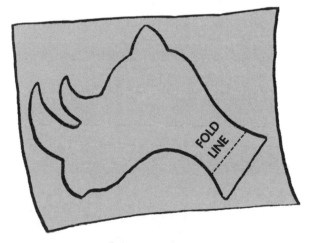

FOLD LINE

Use the marker to draw on the rhino's eyes, mouth, ears, and wrinkles.

3. Bend forward a tab on the rhino's neck and slide it under the cereal-box lid.

Tape the lid closed. Cut out the rhino's tail from construction paper and tape to the box.

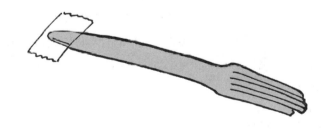

Little Hands Story Corner™

Read "How the Rhinoceros Got His Skin" from Rudyard Kipling's *Just So Stories*.

Ask the Zookeeper

Q: The rhino's horn looks strange and dangerous. What's it made of?

A: Believe it or not, the horn of a rhino is made from the same stuff that's in our fingernails and toenails. It's hard to believe that the horns don't break like our fingernails do!

Getting to Know Us

Try some tools. Rhinos use their horns to dig up tasty bulbs. Try using tools such as a wooden spoon, plastic shovel, or a paper cup to dig. Which tool works the best? Now, use the tool you were born with!

I look like a horse with
stripes black and white,
Which makes me
a rather unusual sight.

Am I a zebra? A panda bear?
A whale?

What you need:

- Tall cardboard tissue box
- Tape
- Scraps of cereal-box cardboard
- Scissors (for grown-up use only)
- Child safety scissors
- Black marker
- Scrap of black construction paper

ENDANGERED

Zebra

What you do:

ASK AN
ADULT TO
CUT HERE

1. Open up the tissue box so it lies flat. Re-form the box so it is inside out. Tape to hold. Tape a scrap of cardboard over the hole in the box. Ask a grown-up to cut a slit in one side of the box.

2. Cut out the neck and head of the zebra from the scrap cardboard.

3. Insert the zebra's neck into the slit. Tape to hold. Cut out the zebra's tail from the black paper and tape it to the box.

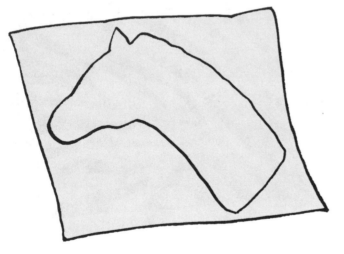

Use the marker to draw the zebra's stripes, eyes, nose, and mouth.

Little Hands Story Corner™

To learn more about zebras, read *The Zebra: Striped Horse* by Christine Denis-Huot.

Q: Why do zebras have stripes?

A: The zebra's stripes help it hide from lions and other animals that might want to eat it. This is called *camouflage*—when the color of your skin or coat disguises you. From far away, a herd of zebras looks like a wild and crazy bunch of stripes instead of a tasty meal. What a clever way to hide!

Getting to Know Us

Now you see us; now you don't. A zebra's stripes run *vertically* (up and down). Draw vertical black stripes on white paper. Bring the paper outdoors and hold it up to see how a striped animal blends into its surroundings. Then, hold the paper so the stripes run *horizontally* (side to side). Would the zebra blend in as well?

One of a kind. Although they may look alike, zebras each have their own patterns. Press your finger onto an ink pad; then, print your fingerprint on paper. Compare your fingerprint with those of family and friends. Are any two fingerprints alike?

Baby zebra! To make a baby zebra, follow the directions above using a ¾ oz (21 g) cereal box.

Tropical Forest

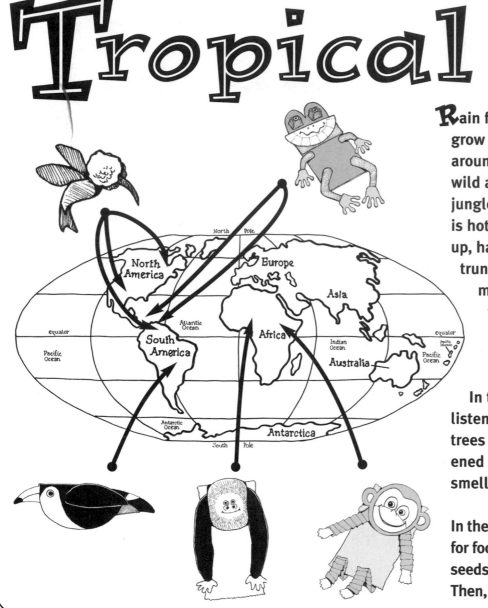

Rain forests, or jungles, are dense, steamy forests that grow in the tropics near the *equator* (an imaginary line around the middle of the earth). Half of all the world's wild animals live here. Animals live everywhere in the jungle. Some creatures live on the forest floor, where it is hot and dark. Some live in the tree branches higher up, hanging on thick vines between the towering tree trunks. (Doesn't that sound like fun?) But most animals in the jungle live right at the tops of the trees, where they find plenty of sunlight and leaves, flowers, fruits, and insects to eat. Some of these animals *never* come down!

In the tropical rain forest habitat at the zoo, you can listen to the sounds of birds and insects. There are tall trees and splashing waterfalls. Your senses are awakened because the exhibit looks, sounds, feels, and even smells like a real rain forest!

In the wild, monkeys spend much of their time searching for food. In the zoo, workers hide raisins and sunflower seeds in the grass and tree holes of the monkey habitat. Then, the monkeys can "discover" their own special treats!

26

See me walking
on all fours.
I look for food
on jungle floors.

Am I a chimpanzee? A pig?
A snake?

ENDANGERED

What you need:

- Child safety scissors
- Brown and white construction paper
- Glue stick
- Brown paper lunch bag, folded flat
- Black marker
- Wiggly eyes (optional)

Chimpanzee

What you do:

1. Cut out the chimp's head and ears from the brown paper. Glue the ears onto the head.

2. Glue the chimp's head onto the flap of the bag. Cut out the chimp's face and the centers of the ears from the white paper. Glue the face onto the head and the centers onto the ears. Use the marker to draw the chimp's nose, mouth, and eyes (or glue on the wiggly eyes).

3. Cut out the chimp's hands and feet from the white paper.

4. Cut out four long strips of brown paper and accordion fold them.

Glue the strips onto the bag for the chimp's arms and legs. Glue on the hands and feet.

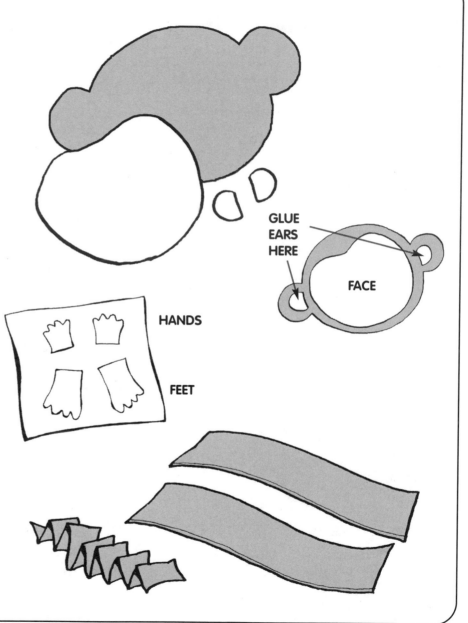

GLUE EARS HERE

FACE

HANDS

FEET

To find out more about these wild and crazy critters,
read *To Be a Chimpanzee* by Chris and Martin Kratt.

Ask the Zookeeper

Q: Are chimps and monkeys the same?

A: They sure do look the same, don't they? But there are some
differences that you might not notice. Chimps belong to the
same family of animals as gorillas (page 36). The animals in
this family are larger than animals in the monkey family.
Chimps and gorillas have no tails, either, but monkeys do.
Chimps are smarter than monkeys are, and that's because
they have bigger brains!

Getting to Know Us

A moving tool. Chimps are very smart. They can make their own tools. When they
get hungry, they poke sticks into termite mounds. Then, they slowly pull up the
termite-covered sticks for a tasty snack.

Here's a tool you can make to move your toys from place to place. Lay a small blanket
on the floor. Pile the toys in the center of the blanket. Hold two corners of the blanket
and pull the toys to wherever you want to go. It's a good way to clean up, too.

I'm the tiniest bird
that you'll ever see.
A red flower's nectar
is a sweet treat for me.

Am I a hummingbird? A rhinoceros?
A bald eagle?

Site: most widely distributed in South America. The ruby-throated hummingbird breeds in eastern North America from Nova Scotia to Florida. The rufous hummingbird breeds from southeastern Alaska to northern California.

What you need:

- Child safety scissors
- Scraps of pink, red, and orange construction paper
- Glue stick
- Light-colored construction paper
- Green marker
- Green pom-pom

Hummingbird

1. Cut out pink, red, and orange paper flowers and glue them onto the light-colored paper. Use the marker to draw leaves and vines.

2. Glue the pom-pom onto the paper for the hummingbird's head. Use the marker to draw the hummingbird's body, wings, tail, and beak.

Little Hands Story Corner™

Read a wonderful legend from Guatemala, *The Hummingbird King*, retold by Argentina Palacios, or *The Great Kapok Tree: A Tale of the African Rain Forest* by Lynne Cherry.

Hmmm... Hmmm...

Ask the Zookeeper

Q: Why are they called hummingbirds? Do they sing a birdsong or hum?

A: Hummingbirds don't hum from their throats, but their wings hum. The birds are named after the "humming" sound their wings make from flapping so fast!

Getting to Know Us

Fast flyers. Hummingbirds fly by moving their wings backward and forward in the shape of an eight, up to 55 times a second. Try moving your arms in a figure eight. How many figure eights can you make in one second?

See my beautiful
bulging red eyes.
I sit in the treetops
feasting on flies.

Am I a red-eyed tree frog? A lion? A panda bear?

What you need:

- Child safety scissors
- Blue, orange, and green construction paper
- Scissors (for grown-up use only)
- Cardboard egg carton
- Brown paper lunch bag, folded flat
- Glue stick
- Small white paper plate
- Stapler
- Red marker
- Tacky glue (available at craft stores)

Red-Eyed Tree Frog

What you do:

1. Cut out the frog's arms and legs from the blue paper. Cut out its hands and feet from the orange paper. To make the frog's eyes, cut two half-circles from the green paper. Ask a grown-up to cut out two egg-carton sections.

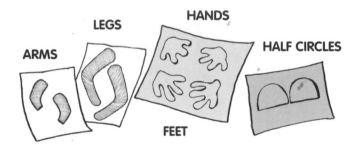

ARMS LEGS HANDS HALF CIRCLES FEET

2. Place the paper bag so the bottom flap is at the top. Glue on the green paper to cover the front of the bag, gluing it under the flap.

3. To make the frog's mouth, fold the paper plate in half and staple it to the flap with the round side down. Use the marker to draw the frog's mouth.

4. For the eyes, glue the green half-circles to the top of the bag, tucking them behind the paper plate.

Color the egg-carton sections red; then, use the tacky glue to glue them onto the green half-circles.

5. Glue the frog's arms and legs onto the front of the bag. Glue on the hands and feet.

Little Hands Story Corner™

Read *Frog on His Own* by Mercer Mayer.

Ask the Zookeeper

Q: I've never seen a frog in a tree. Are you sure the red-eyed tree frog lives in trees? Maybe they just live *near* trees.

A: Yup, the red-eyed tree frog really lives *in* trees, but you won't see it unless you visit the rain forests of Central or South America! The red-eyed tree frogs have special suction pads at the ends of their toes that help them climb trees and cling to branches and leaves. Wouldn't it be fun if you could live in the treetops?

Getting to Know Us

Color me happy! Red-eyed tree frogs can change color—from a darker green to a reddish-brown, depending on their moods. What color do you feel like when you're happy? What color do you feel like when you're sad? Angry?

Nicknames. Red-eyed tree frogs are also called "monkey frogs" because of their great coordination and climbing skills. Do you have a nickname? What does your nickname say about you?

...gning is something
...hat I can be taught.
... may look ferocious,
...ut I really am not.

Am I a dolphin? A mouse? A gorilla?

ENDANGERED

What you need:

- Child safety scissors
- Small white paper plate
- Black construction paper
- Scrap of white construction paper
- Glue stick
- Black marker
- Wiggly eyes (optional)
- Paper lunch bag (brown or white), folded flat

Gorilla

Site: tropical forests of West Africa

What you do:

1. To make the head, cut away the sides of the paper plate. Cut out the gorilla's arms from the black paper. Cut out hands from the white paper and glue them at the ends of the arms.

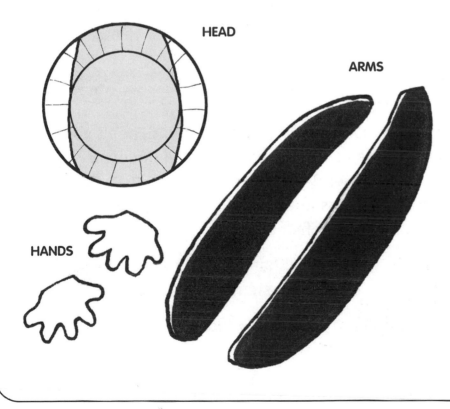

HEAD

ARMS

HANDS

2. Use the marker to draw the gorilla's hair and face (or glue on the wiggly eyes).

3. Glue the gorilla's head and arms to the flap of the bag.

Little Hands Story Corner™

Read *Good Night, Gorilla* by Peggy Rathmann.

Q: When I see gorillas in cartoons, they're always beating their chests. How come they do that?

A: Gorillas beat their chests to make themselves seem strong and fierce. This scares away their enemies. Do you think they're fierce when they do that, or do you think they're funny?

Getting to Know Us

Do the knuckle walk. When they're on the ground, adult gorillas walk with the knuckles of their hands curled under so they're in front of their feet. Try walking like a gorilla. Squat down and bend your fingers under so you can drag your hands on the ground. Can you walk fast or slow?

Meet Koko. Koko is a gorilla that has learned to use American Sign Language. Here's one way to sign "I love you."

To learn more about Koko, go to <**http://koko.org/world/**>.

Something about me is unique. It's the size of my big, beautiful, bright yellow beak.

Am I a giraffe? A toucan? A rooster?

What you need:

- Child safety scissors
- Large white paper plate
- Black construction paper
- Tape
- Black and yellow markers
- Glue stick
- Scraps of white, red, and yellow construction paper

Toucan

What you do:

1. Fold the paper plate in half and cut out the center. Cut out the toucan's tail from the black paper and tape it inside the folded plate.

2. Use the black marker to color the plate. Use the black and yellow markers for the toucan's eyes.

3. Cut out the toucan's wings from the black paper and glue one onto each side of the plate. Cut out white and red paper feathers and glue them onto the black tail.

4. Cut out the toucan's bill from the yellow paper and tape it inside the plate.

Tape the plate closed.

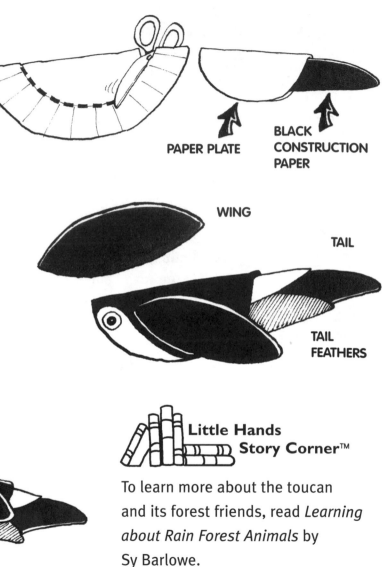

PAPER PLATE

BLACK CONSTRUCTION PAPER

WING

TAIL

TAIL FEATHERS

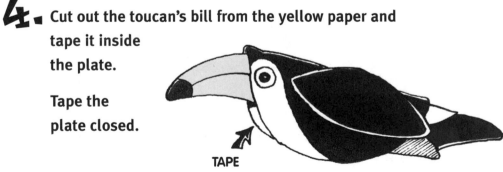

TAPE

Little Hands Story Corner™

To learn more about the toucan and its forest friends, read *Learning about Rain Forest Animals* by Sy Barlowe.

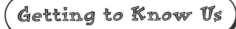
Eat toucan-style! Toucans pick up food in the tips of their large *bills* (beaks), then toss their heads back and catch the morsels in their mouths. Without using your hands, try putting a cookie into your mouth. Would it be easier or harder if you had a bill?

Tight as a toucan. Toucans nest in tree holes. How do you think they fit into the bottom of tight-fitting holes? They bend double: They twist their bills around and rest them on their backs; then, they fold their tails up on to their chests, and their wings wrap around the rest of their bodies. How small a ball can you curl up into?

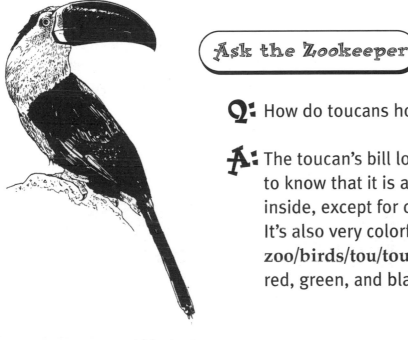

Ask the Zookeeper

Q: How do toucans hold up their heads with such large bills?

A: The toucan's bill looks very heavy, I agree. It might surprise you to know that it is actually very light because it's almost all hollow inside, except for crisscrossed pieces of bone that make it strong. It's also very colorful. Visit the website <**www.belizezoo.org/zoo/zoo/birds/tou/tou1.html**> to see a toucan with its huge yellow, red, green, and black bill.

Animals & Their Young

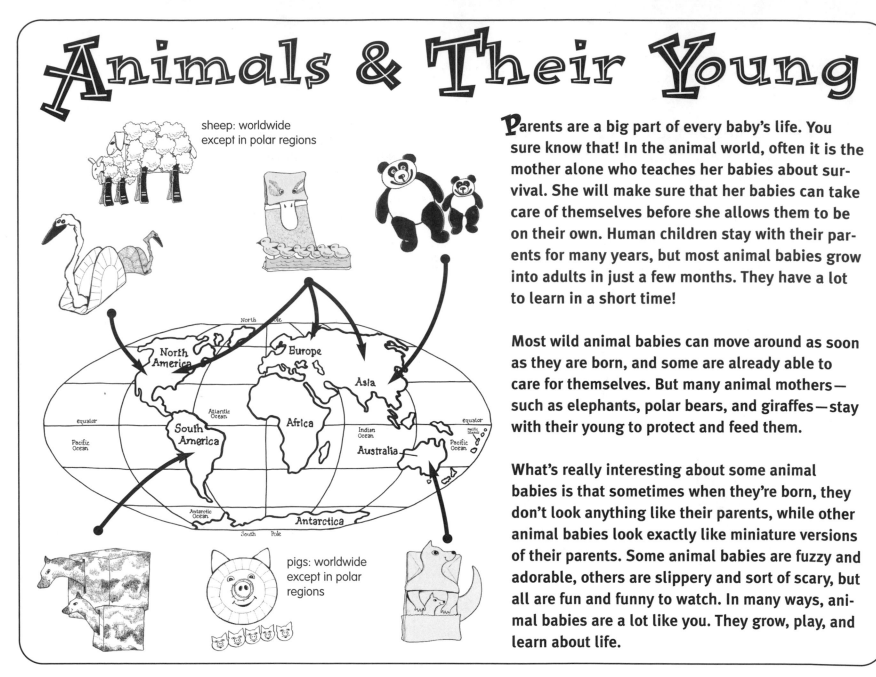

sheep: worldwide except in polar regions

pigs: worldwide except in polar regions

Parents are a big part of every baby's life. You sure know that! In the animal world, often it is the mother alone who teaches her babies about survival. She will make sure that her babies can take care of themselves before she allows them to be on their own. Human children stay with their parents for many years, but most animal babies grow into adults in just a few months. They have a lot to learn in a short time!

Most wild animal babies can move around as soon as they are born, and some are already able to care for themselves. But many animal mothers—such as elephants, polar bears, and giraffes—stay with their young to protect and feed them.

What's really interesting about some animal babies is that sometimes when they're born, they don't look anything like their parents, while other animal babies look exactly like miniature versions of their parents. Some animal babies are fuzzy and adorable, others are slippery and sort of scary, but all are fun and funny to watch. In many ways, animal babies are a lot like you. They grow, play, and learn about life.

Look in my pouch
and guess what you'll see?
That's right —
it's a mini-version of me.

Am I a kangaroo? A robin?
A crocodile?

What you need:

- Brown paper lunch bag
- Child safety scissors
- Brown construction paper
- Glue stick
- Brown marker

Kangaroo and Joey

What you do:

1. Fold down the top of the bag. Turn the bag upside down so the fold becomes a pocket; fold the bag flat.

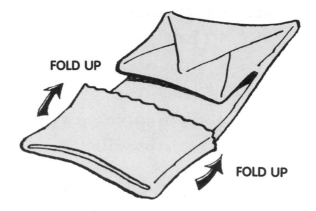

FOLD UP

FOLD UP

2. Cut out the head and shoulders of the kangaroo from the brown paper.

Glue the shoulders onto the flap.

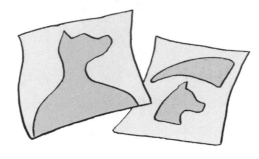

3. Cut out a small kangaroo head and neck from the brown paper and glue it inside the pocket. Cut out a tail and glue it to the side of the bag.

4. Use the marker to draw each kangaroo's eyes, nose, and mouth. Draw arms on the mother kangaroo.

Q: Why do kangaroos hop? They look so funny when they do!

A: Nobody knows for sure why kangaroos hop instead of running on all fours. One reason could be that kangaroo babies are less likely to fall out of the pouches if mama kangaroos stand up straight to hop. What do you think? Make up your own story about why kangaroos hop.

Getting to Know Us

Kangaroo puppet. Kangaroos use their *hind* (back) legs to hop. Put your hand inside the paper bag and move your hand up and down so your kangaroo puppet "hops" along a tabletop. Now, lean over slightly and hop on two feet, jumping forward kangaroo-style.

Baby Kangaroo!

A baby kangaroo, a *joey*, is carried in a pouch on its mother's belly. For several weeks, the joey stays hidden inside the pouch, sleeping and *nursing* (drinking milk). In three months, the young kangaroo is big enough to climb down to the ground and nibble on grass. The joey is ready to leave the pouch for good after about nine months.

Ask a grown-up if you could crawl or walk when you were nine months old.

**Little Hands
Story Corner**™

Read *Katy No-Pocket* by Emmy Payne.

Gliding on water,
I can be found,
Lovely and graceful,
with fluffy white down.

Am I a swan? A frog? A goose?

Site: the Pacific Coast, Rocky Mountains, and the interior of northwestern North America

ENDANGERED

What you need:

- 2 pipe cleaners
- Child safety scissors
- White tissue paper
- Ruler
- Glue stick
- Scrap of black construction paper
- Black marker
- Large white paper plate
- Tape

Trumpeter Swan and Cygnet

What you do:

1. Twist together the two pipe cleaners end to end. Cut a strip of tissue paper 3" (7.5 cm) wide and slightly longer than the pipe-cleaner stem. Place the pipe-cleaner stem in the center of the tissue paper; then, fold the tissue paper over the stem a couple of times to make a strip 1" (2.5 cm) wide.

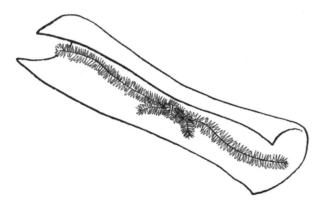

Press the tissue paper down flat and glue along its length.

2. Cut out the swan's beak from the black paper and glue it onto one end of the tissue-paper strip.

Draw the swan's black eyes.

3. Bend the tissue-paper strip into the shape of a swan's neck. Fold up two sides of the paper plate and tape the swan's neck in between.

Tape the edges of the plate together.

**Little Hands
Story Corner**™

Read *The Trumpet of the Swan* by E. B. White or *The Ugly Duckling* by Hans Christian Andersen.

Ask the Zookeeper

Q: Can the trumpeter swan play the trumpet?

A: No, but it sounds as if it is playing one! The trumpeter swan is named for the sound it makes, which is deep and musical, like a trumpet. It sounds like *ko-hoh, ko-hoh, ko-hoh*. Which musical instrument does your voice sound like?

Getting to Know Us

Dancing swans. Visit your local library for a video of the ballet *Swan Lake*. Watch the graceful dancers move around on stage. Do they look like swans? Now, you dance to the music, too.

Baby Swan!

Baby swans are called *cygnets* (SIG-nets). When they are very young, they climb onto their mother's or father's back to snuggle in the warm feathers. Then, they cruise around the pond as though they're riding on a boat! (Have you ever done that on the back of a grown-up swimmer?) When they're born, cygnets aren't the same color as their parents.

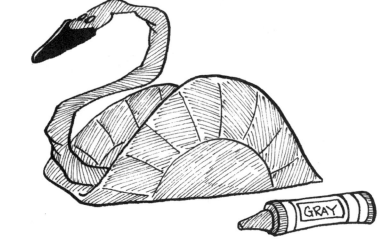

To make a cygnet, follow the same directions on pages 47–48, only use a small white paper plate and one pipe cleaner. Use a gray crayon to color the cygnet.

I'm black and white,
and I eat bamboo.
You can see me
in a zoo.

ENDANGERED

Site: forests of western and central China

Am I a penguin? A rooster? A panda?

What you need:

- Salt clay (recipe on page 52)
- Cookie sheet (optional)
- Black and white tempera paints, in dishes or lids
- Small paintbrush

Giant Panda Bear and Cub

What you do:

Salt Clay

¾ cup (175 ml) table salt
2 cups (500 ml) flour
Bowl
¾ cup (175 ml) water
Spoon

To make this self-hardening clay, mix the salt and flour in the bowl. Then, gradually add the water. When the clay forms a ball around the spoon, *knead* (work with your hands) the clay, adding a little water if it gets too crumbly.

1. Roll a ball of clay for the panda's body. Roll a smaller ball for the panda's head. Press the balls together, then, use your palm to flatten them.

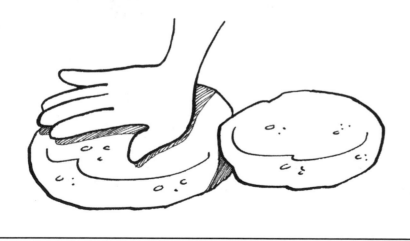

2. Roll two short fat tubes of clay for the legs and two longer, thinner tubes for the arms. From the ends of the arms, pinch off small pieces for the panda's ears, nose, eyes, and mouth and press them onto the head.

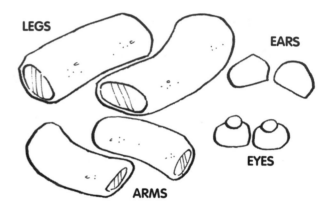

LEGS

EARS

ARMS

EYES

Then, press the tubes onto the panda for arms and legs.

3. Ask a grown-up to help bake the panda in the oven at 300°F (150°C) for 30 to 40 minutes or until hard, or allow it to air dry. Paint the panda black and white.

Q: Why is a giant panda bear black and white? It looks so funny with all of the different parts of color on it.

A: You might think that the bold colors on a panda would make it very easy to see in the forest. In fact, panda bears live in the mountains around a lot of snow and rock, so their black and white coats provide camouflage from animals that hunt them. Can you think of another black and white animal you've met that uses camouflage to remain safe from enemies? If you guessed a zebra (page 23), you were correct!

Getting to Know Us

Visit us! Check out the live web cams on these websites to see real panda bears at the Smithsonian National Zoo and the San Diego Zoo: <http://pandas.si.edu/index.htm> and <http://www.sandiegozoo.org/special/pandas/pandacam/index.html>.

Have a panda bear party. Use black and white decorations, serve a panda bear cake, and make "black and white" ice cream floats (floating vanilla ice cream in chocolate milk).

Baby Panda!

Even though giant pandas grow to weigh about 220 pounds (100 kg), they are very tiny when they're born as panda cubs. They actually look like little white rats (without tails, of course!), and they weigh only about 4 ounces (125 g). That's a lot less than you weighed when you were born! For the first couple of months, their mothers care for them by holding them to their chests with their large front paws.

Use the salt clay to make a little panda cub for your big panda bear.

Little Hands Story Corner™

Read *Little Panda: The World Welcomes Hua Mei at the San Diego Zoo* by Joanne Ryder, or watch the video *The Amazing Panda Adventure*, a story about a boy and girl who rescue a panda cub from hunters.

This two-toed
woolly mammal
Looks like
a humpless camel.

Am I a crow? A llama? A wolf?

Site: western South America, mostly Bolivia, Chile, and Peru

What you need:

- Tall cardboard tissue box
- Tape
- Scraps of cereal-box cardboard
- Scissors (for grown-up use only)
- Child safety scissors
- Black marker
- Sponge
- White, black, and brown tempera paints, in dishes or lids

Llama and Cria

What you do:

1. Open up the tissue box so it lies flat. Re-form the box so it is inside out. Tape to hold. Tape a scrap of cardboard over the hole in the box. Ask a grown-up to cut a slit in the bottom of the box.

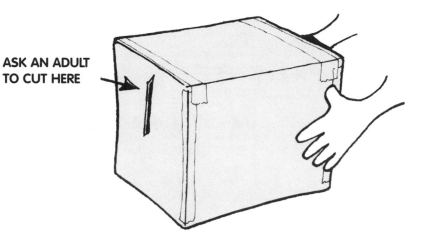

ASK AN ADULT TO CUT HERE

2. Cut out the llama's head and neck from the scrap cardboard.

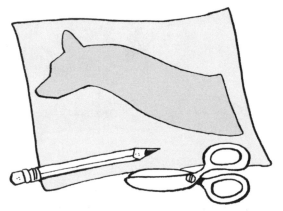

Use the marker to draw on the llama's eyes and mouth.

3. Dab the sponge into one of the paints. Press it onto the llama's head and body for hair. Let dry. Repeat with the remaining colors.

4. Fold a tab at the end of the llama's neck and insert it into the slit. Tape to hold.

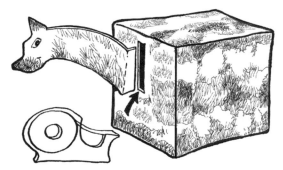

Little Hands Story Corner™

Read *Is Your Mama a Llama?* by Deborah Guarino.

Ask the Zookeeper

Q: We were at a petting zoo, and a llama spit at my sister. Yuck! Why did it do that?

A: Most of the time, llamas spit at *each other*, not at people. That's one way that mama llamas discipline their crias—by spitting at them! They also spit if they're fighting over food or feeling uncomfortable when people or other llamas are "invading their space." What do you do when you want to be left alone? (Not spit, I hope!)

Getting to Know Us

Make a herd of llamas. Llamas come in a variety of colors, from white to black, along with many shades of brown. Make several cereal-box llamas using different colors of paint. Let them "graze" along your bookcase or windowsill.

Baby Llama!

A baby llama is called a *cria* (CREE-a). When it is born, it is covered with curly wool that grows into a thick, warm coat. The cria's coat is often a different color from its mother's coat. (That's like you having blond hair when your mother has brown hair.)

To make a cria, follow the same directions on pages 55–56 using a ¾ oz (21 g) cereal box. Perhaps you will want to use a different color paint for your cria.

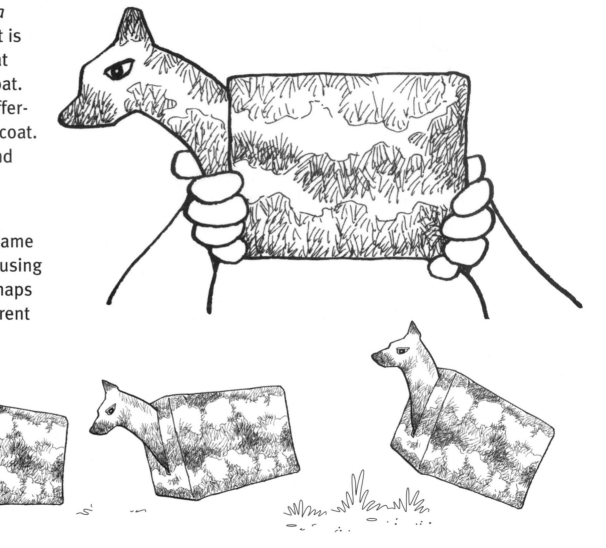

Guess who I am.
Here is a clue:
My warm woolen coat
makes a sweater for "ewe."

Am I a sheep? An owl? A mouse?

What you need:

- Toilet-paper tube
- White paper
- Tape
- Glue stick
- Cotton balls
- Child safety scissors
- Black marker
- 2 spring-clip clothespins

Sheep and Lamb

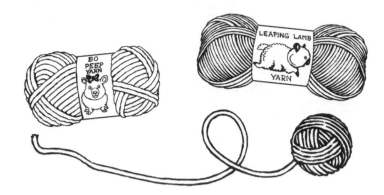

1. Wrap the tube in the white paper and tape to hold.

2. Flatten the tube. Cut out the ears, head, and tail from the white paper and glue them onto the sheep. Then, glue on the cotton balls.

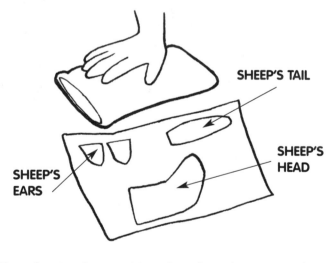

SHEEP'S TAIL

SHEEP'S HEAD

SHEEP'S EARS

Use the marker to draw the sheep's eyes and mouth.

3. Color the clothespins with the black marker for the legs. Clip the clothespins onto the tube to stand the sheep upright.

Ask the Zookeeper

Q: How much wool does a sheep have?

A: Would you believe that an average Shropshire *ram* (male sheep) has 10 to 14 pounds (4.5 to 6.5 kg) of wool? (That's about how much a human baby weighs when it is two weeks old!) And every pound (g) of wool can make 10 miles (16 km) of yarn. That's a lot of wool sweaters! In case you are wondering, it doesn't hurt the sheep to be sheared. In fact, shearing can make the sheep more comfortable.

Getting to Know Us

Sing a song. Learn the words to the song "Baa, Baa, Black Sheep."

Baby Sheep!

A baby sheep is called a *lamb*. The first sound it makes is a soft *ma-a-a-a* (which becomes *ba-a-a-a* after the lamb grows up). The mother sheep answers with her own special call. From then on, the mother sheep and her lamb can recognize each other's voices.

To make a lamb, follow the same directions on pages 59–60, using a toilet-paper tube that has been cut in half by a grown-up. Cut the shapes shown here to finish your lamb.

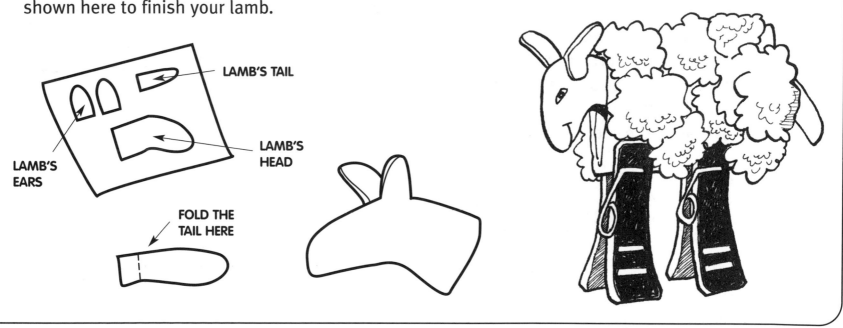

ASK AN
ADULT TO
CUT HERE

LAMB'S TAIL

LAMB'S EARS

LAMB'S HEAD

FOLD THE
TAIL HERE

My pen is a mess.
I like it that way.
"Oink, oink"
is all I ever say.

Am I a raccoon? An elephant? A pig?

What you need:

- White and red tempera paints
- Paintbrush
- Paper drinking cup (nonwaxed)
- Black marker
- Large white paper plate
- Pencil
- Scissors (for grown-up use only)
- Child safety scissors
- Scrap of pink construction paper
- Tape
- Popsicle stick

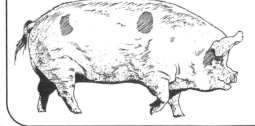

Pig and Piglets

What you do:

1. Mix a few drops of red paint into the white paint in a dish or lid for pink. Paint the bottom half of the paper cup pink. Let dry. Use the marker to draw the pig's nose on the bottom of the cup.

2. Paint the paper plate pink. Let dry.

3. Place the cup, upright, in the center of the plate, and trace around the bottom. Ask a grown-up to help cut out the circle. Cut small slits around the circle.

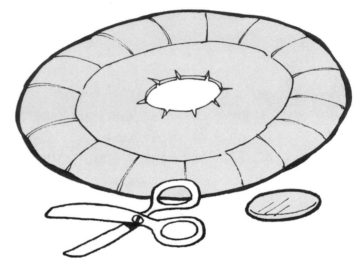

4. Cut out the pig's ears from the pink paper and tape them onto the plate. Use the marker to draw the pig's eyes and mouth on the plate. Insert the pig's nose through the hole in the plate. Tape to hold.

5. Tape the stick onto the back of the plate to make a pig puppet.

**Little Hands
Story Corner**™

Rent the video *Babe* for a story about a little pig on a farm in England, or read *The Little Pig* by Judy Dunn.

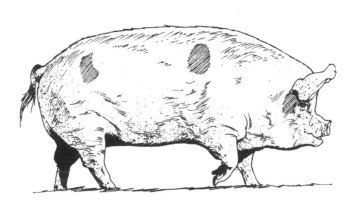

Ask the Zookeeper

Q: Why are pigs always lying in the mud? Do they like getting dirty all the time?

A: Pigs aren't really any dirtier than other animals. It's just that like many other animals, pigs like to take baths in mud. The mud keeps them cool on hot days and protects their skin from pesky insects. What would you think about taking a bath in mud?

Getting to Know Us

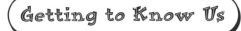

Animal families. A mother pig is called a *sow* (sounds like *ow!*). She has about 14 piglets at a time! When so many babies are born to animals at one time, the group of babies is called a *litter*. If you know anyone whose dog or cat has had babies lately, ask how many babies were in the litter.

Baby Pig!

Baby pigs, called *piglets*, stand up and walk around as soon as they are born. They grunt and squeal as they feed on their mother's milk. In a few weeks, they can eat grain and vegetable scraps. To make a family of piglets, cut out piglet heads from pink construction paper. Use a black marker to draw on the eyes, nose, and mouth.

Cut a piece of pink paper 1" x 2" (2.5 x 5 cm). Roll it up into a tube and tape the back to hold.

ACTUAL SIZE

Glue the faces to the tube as shown.

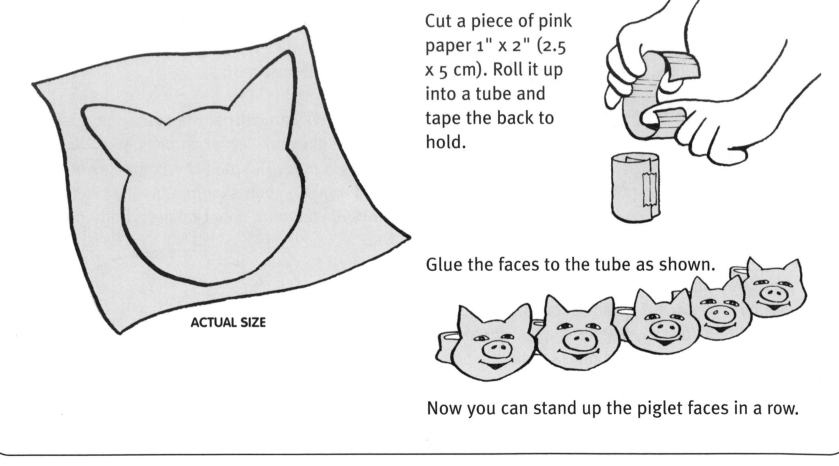

Now you can stand up the piglet faces in a row.

Look for me by the pond
and you may find
My little ducklings
waddling behind.

Am I a bald eagle? A blue jay? A duck?

What you need:

- Scraps of yellow, green, and white construction paper
- Child safety scissors
- Brown paper lunch bag, folded flat
- Glue stick
- Green and brown markers
- Wiggly eyes (optional)

Mallard Duck and Ducklings

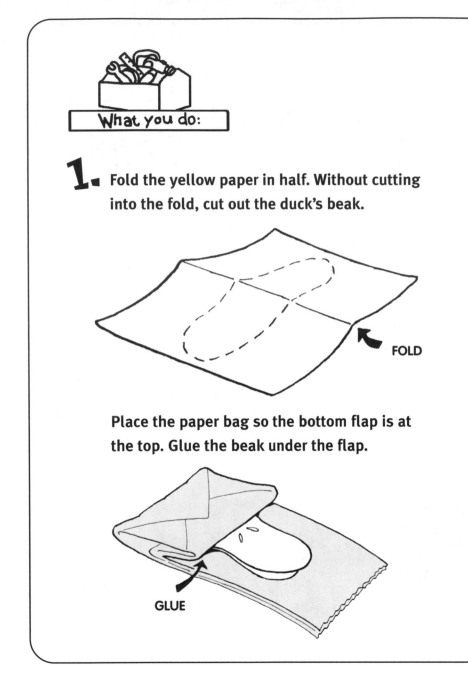

What you do:

1. Fold the yellow paper in half. Without cutting into the fold, cut out the duck's beak.

FOLD

Place the paper bag so the bottom flap is at the top. Glue the beak under the flap.

GLUE

2. Glue green paper over the flap of the bag. Use the green marker to color the area under the flap. Glue a strip of white paper across the duck's neck on either side of the beak.

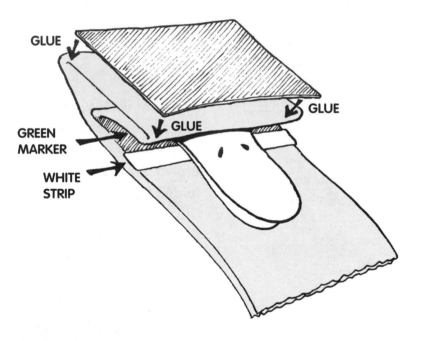

GLUE

GLUE

GREEN MARKER

GLUE

WHITE STRIP

3. Use the brown marker to draw the duck's feathers on the bag. Draw eyes (or glue on wiggly eyes).

Q: I see baby ducks floating around on ponds and lakes while they're still so little. How did they learn to swim?

A: Good question! Young ducklings learn things through *imprinting* (copying what they see something else do). Ducklings follow the first moving object they see, which is the mother duck. By watching her, they learn what to do. Does this sound like the way you learn new things?

Getting to Know Us

Different-colored ducks. Mother mallards (*hens*) are a dull color compared to the male mallard (*drake*). The male duck has a glossy green head and white-ringed neck, while the hen is brown and black. The ducklings are brown, too. This helps the mother and ducklings hide in the reeds so other animals can't find the ducklings to eat them. Can you think of other animal babies that are a different color from their parents? If you said baby swan (page 50), you were correct!

Play duck, duck, goose. Sit in a circle with your friends. One player walks around the outside of the circle, lightly tapping each player on the head. With each tap, she says "duck." Then, she taps one player and says "goose." The "goose" stands up and runs around the circle to catch the player who tapped him. If the player can sit in the "goose's" space before being tagged, the "goose" becomes the new player to go around the circle. If the "goose" tags the original player, the original player starts the game again.

Baby Duck!

Baby ducks, called *duck-lings*, are born with *down* (very soft, fluffy feathers). In a few weeks, they lose their down and grow a new set of feathers. Here's how to make ducklings: Ask a grown-up to cut an egg carton in half the long way. Cut out ducklings and a *hen* (mother duck) from

brown construction paper. Turn the egg carton upside down and glue a strip of blue paper onto one side for water. Tape a toothpick to the back of the hen and each duckling. Line up the duck-lings behind their mother by poking each toothpick through the top of an egg section.

Little Hands Story Corner™

Go to the library and take out the CD *Peter and the Wolf*. Listen for the part of the duck. Or, read *Make Way for Ducklings* by Robert McCloskey.

Inside the Aquarium

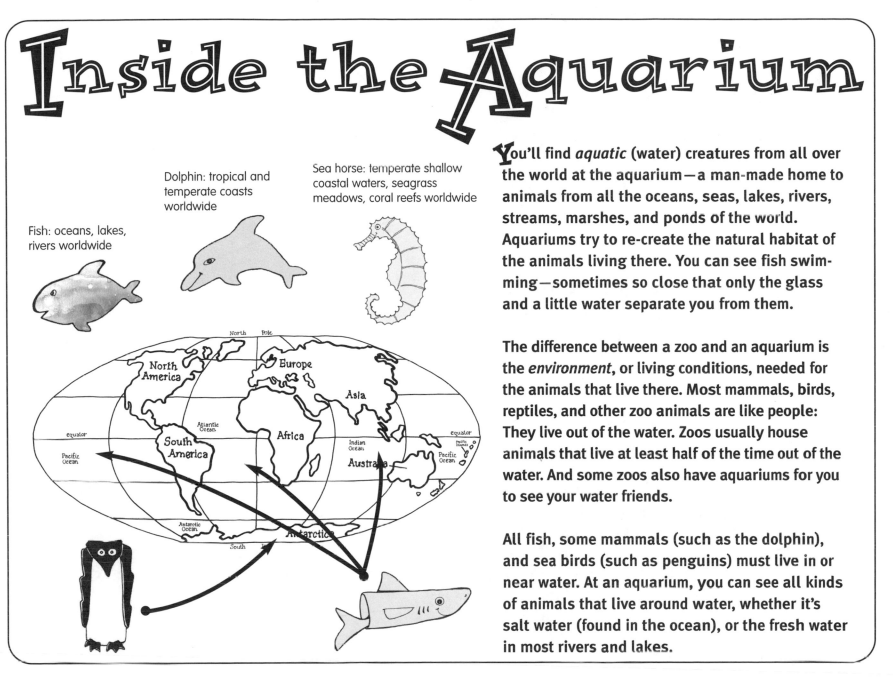

Fish: oceans, lakes, rivers worldwide

Dolphin: tropical and temperate coasts worldwide

Sea horse: temperate shallow coastal waters, seagrass meadows, coral reefs worldwide

North Pole

North America

Europe

Asia

Atlantic Ocean

equator

Pacific Ocean

South America

Africa

Indian Ocean

Pacific Islands

equator

Pacific Ocean

Australia

Antarctic Ocean

Antarctica

South Pole

You'll find *aquatic* (water) creatures from all over the world at the aquarium—a man-made home to animals from all the oceans, seas, lakes, rivers, streams, marshes, and ponds of the world. Aquariums try to re-create the natural habitat of the animals living there. You can see fish swimming—sometimes so close that only the glass and a little water separate you from them.

The difference between a zoo and an aquarium is the *environment*, or living conditions, needed for the animals that live there. Most mammals, birds, reptiles, and other zoo animals are like people: They live out of the water. Zoos usually house animals that live at least half of the time out of the water. And some zoos also have aquariums for you to see your water friends.

All fish, some mammals (such as the dolphin), and sea birds (such as penguins) must live in or near water. At an aquarium, you can see all kinds of animals that live around water, whether it's salt water (found in the ocean), or the fresh water in most rivers and lakes.

Fish in the ocean
fear me because —
There is no escape
when I open my jaws.

Am I a starfish? A shark? A bald eagle?

What you need:

- Cardboard tube, any size
- Blue construction paper
- Tape
- Child safety scissors
- Black marker
- Wiggly eyes (optional)
- Glue stick (optional)

Shark

What you do:

1. Cover the tube with the blue paper and tape to hold. Cut out four shark fins from the blue paper. Tape two fins onto the sides of the tube. Tape the dorsal fin onto the top of the tube. Tape the tail fin inside one end of the tube.

2. Cut out a mountain shape from the blue paper and tape it around the opposite end of the tube for the shark's head.

3. Use the marker to draw the shark's mouth and gills. Draw eyes (or glue on the wiggly eyes).

TAIL FIN

DORSAL FIN
FOR TOP

2 SIDE FINS

MOUNTAIN SHAPE
FOR HEAD

Q: Sometimes I've seen little fish swim away so fast. What about big fish? Can a big, fat shark keep up with a quick, little fish?

A: A shark is one of the fastest fish alive. It can swim up to 60 miles (97 km) per hour! The next time you're in the car with a grown-up, ask her to tell you when she's driving 60 miles (97 km) per hour. That's how fast a shark can swim. It might even beat you to the grocery store!

Getting to Know Us

Sharp shark teeth. Sharks have rows of sharp teeth. Draw a picture of a shark with its mouth wide open. Glue uncooked rice onto your drawing to look like the shark's teeth.

The nose knows. A shark's sense of smell is so powerful that it can smell things in the water many yards (m) away. Name some things you like to smell. What don't you like to smell?

I swim in a school
but don't learn to read.
A large, salty ocean
is all that I need.

Am I a fish? An anteater?
A seashell?

What you need:

- Paintbrush
- Watercolor paints
- Sheet of white paper
- Child safety scissors
- 2 sheets of blue
  construction paper
- Tape
- Glue stick
- Black marker

Site: oceans, freshwater lakes, and rivers all over the world

Fish

What you do:

Little Hands Story Corner™

Read *Fish Wish* by Bob Barner.

1. Paint the entire sheet of white paper with watercolors, allowing the colors to run together. Let dry.

2. Cut out fish shapes from the painted sheet of paper.

3. Tape the two sheets of blue paper end to end. Glue on the fish shapes.

4. Use the marker to draw waves and air bubbles.

Smart fish. Ask a grown-up to cut out a fish shape from a sponge. Pour a small amount of tempera paint into a dish or lid. Dab the sponge into the paint and press onto paper for a school of fish.

Play go fish! Each player gets five cards, facedown. The remaining cards go in a "fish pile." The first player asks another player for a card that has the same number as one of the cards in her hand. If the second player has a card with that number, he must give it to the player who asked for it. She can put this pair of matching cards aside and ask another player for a card that matches one in her hand. If the second player doesn't have it, he can say, "Go fish!" She must take the top card from the fish pile (if it's a match, she can put that pair aside), and the player who said, "Go fish" can start asking other players for cards. The first player to run out of cards is the winner.

Ask the Zookeeper

Q: When fish swim in schools, is there one fish that is the leader, like a teacher?

A: No special fish is the leader. Each fish watches the other ones around it, and then it moves in the same direction and at the same speed. Do you do the same thing when you're out walking with your friends?

People enjoy
swimming with me.
My pointy snout
is plain to see.

Am I a dolphin? A rooster? A horse?

What you need:

- Scissors (for grown-up use only)
- Cereal box, 10 oz (283 g)
- Blue and gray construction paper
- Glue stick
- Child safety scissors
- Black crayon
- Markers, assorted colors

Site: almost all tropical and temperate coasts throughout the world

Dolphin

What you do:

1. Ask a grown-up to help you cut off the top half of the cereal box; then, cut off three-fourths of the front panel. Cut a slit in the bottom of the box.

2. Use the markers to draw fish and seaweed on one sheet of blue paper. Glue the blue paper onto the back panel inside the cereal box. Cut out waves from the blue paper. Glue the waves onto the front of the cereal box.

3. Cut out a dolphin shape from the gray paper. Use the crayon to draw the dolphin's eyes and mouth. From the leftover cardboard, cut a strip about the size of a Popsicle stick. Glue the dolphin onto the top of the strip.

4. Now holding the strip in the slit, play with your dolphin as it glides through the water.

Little Hands Story Corner™

Ask if your local library has the video *Nova: Private Lives of Dolphins* for some wonderful action scenes of dolphins.

Q: My mom buys me tuna fish at the store, and sometimes the can has a picture of a dolphin on it. How come?

A: The dolphin picture tells you that no dolphins were hurt when the tuna were caught in the ocean. You see, some kinds of dolphins like to swim with schools of tuna. When the tuna are caught, the dolphins can easily be hurt. Now, some tuna companies are very careful not to hurt dolphins when they catch tuna. And that's a good thing!

Getting to Know Us

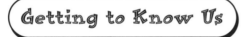

Pucker up. Bottle-nosed dolphins identify themselves with a signature whistle. You can learn to whistle, too. All you need is what you already have—one pair of lips, one set of lungs, and some patience.

Step 1: Shape your lips into a small *O*.
Step 2: Place your tongue behind your lower front teeth.
Step 3: Take a deep breath and let it out, tightening your lips as it goes.

No luck? If the only sound that comes out is air, keep trying. If you practice, you'll be able to whistle a tune!

I never gallop;
I cannot neigh.
I spend all my time
underwater each day.

Am I a seal? A butterfly?
A sea horse?

ENDANGERED

Site: temperate shallow coastal waters, seagrass meadows, coral reefs worldwide

What you need:

- Child safety scissors (wavy-edged scissors optional)
- Small white paper plate
- Black marker
- Glue stick
- Blue and green construction paper
- Sea shells (optional)

Sea Horse

What you do:

1. Cut out the shape of a sea horse from the edge of the paper plate.

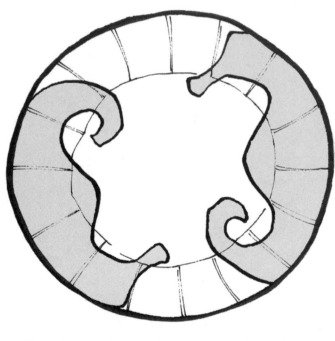

Use the marker to draw the sea horse's eyes and nose.

2. Glue the sea horse onto the blue paper. Tear seaweed shapes from the green paper. Glue them onto the blue paper.

3. Use the marker to draw fish swimming around the sea horse. If you have small shells, glue them to the ocean bottom.

Q: If a sea horse is a fish, why is it called a horse?

A: If you look at a picture of a sea horse and a picture of a real horse, you'll notice one thing in common—a long *snout*. That's where the tip of the nose is. On a horse, this part of the body is called a *muzzle*. Can you think of other animals that have long snouts or muzzles?

Getting to Know Us

Mind your table manners. Sea horses are very noisy eaters. They have no teeth, so they swallow their food whole. They suck up whole shrimp with their long, hollow jaws. What sound do you make when you suck up spaghetti?

Little Hands Story Corner™

Read *One Lonely Sea Horse* by Saxton Freymann.

In cold and ice
I waddle about.
My tuxedo is something
I can't do without.

Am I an owl? A penguin? A sea turtle?

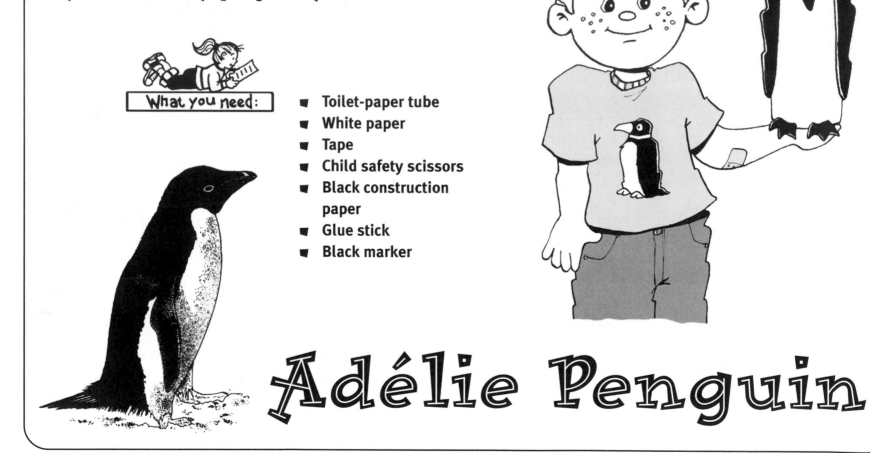

What you need:

- Toilet-paper tube
- White paper
- Tape
- Child safety scissors
- Black construction paper
- Glue stick
- Black marker

Adélie Penguin

What you do:

1. Wrap the tube in the white paper and tape to hold. Cut out the penguin's feet and wings from the black paper. Tape the penguin's feet to the inside front of the tube so they hang below the tube.

WINGS

FEET

2. Cut out a strip 2" x 8" (5 x 20 cm) from the black paper. Cut a point at each end of the black paper strip.

Tape the strip to the back of the tube.

Fold the strip over the top of the tube for the penguin's head and tape along the sides to hold.

FOLD

FOLD

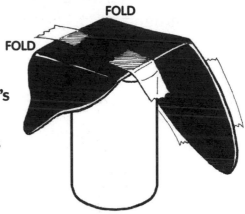

3. Tape the wings to the sides of the tube.

4. Cut out the penguin's eyes from the white paper and glue them on. Use the marker to finish the eyes.

Read *Penguins in the Fridge* by Nicola Moon.

Ask the Zookeeper

Q: Are penguins birds or mammals? They have wings, but they walk around sort of like us.

A: Penguins are birds, but they don't know how to fly. In fact, they waddle around just as some people do. Their wings are actually more like flippers, the kind people use when they're learning to swim. Penguins use their wings to swim very fast. They also use them to keep their balance.

Getting to Know Us

Play penguin dad. The male Emperor penguin carries its mate's single egg at the top of its feet. The egg is held in place by a fold of skin. The female penguin returns about two months later, when the young penguin emerges. Try walking with a hard-boiled egg or a tennis ball balanced on your feet. How far can you get without the egg falling off?

The Reptile House

snake: all seven continents

Let's look at a group of animals called *reptiles*. Snakes, chameleons, lizards, turtles, alligators, and crocodiles are all reptiles. Reptiles are *vertebrate* animals—like mammals and birds, they have a backbone made up of small bones called *vertebrae*. Reptiles are also cold-blooded, which means that their body temperatures change depending on where they live. (You are warm-blooded, and usually your body temperature is 98.6°F/37.3°C whether you're skiing in Canada or sunning in Florida.)

Reptiles live in many kinds of habitats. Some live in trees. A few reptiles live on mountains up to three miles (5 km) above sea level. Others are aquatic, living in fresh water or salt water. Reptiles are also found in deserts, swamps, forests, grasslands, gardens, and maybe even your backyard! Wherever they live, the one thing they all need is sun. That is why they are housed at the zoo in "reptile houses." If the weather outside is cold or rainy, the sunlamps and glass in the house keeps them warm and comfortable.

With no arms or legs,
I slither around.
Listen for
a hissing sound.

Am I a grasshopper? A snake? A horse?

Site: all seven continents

What you need:

- Child safety scissors
- Red, black, and yellow construction paper
- Black pipe cleaner
- Glue stick
- Wiggly eyes (optional)

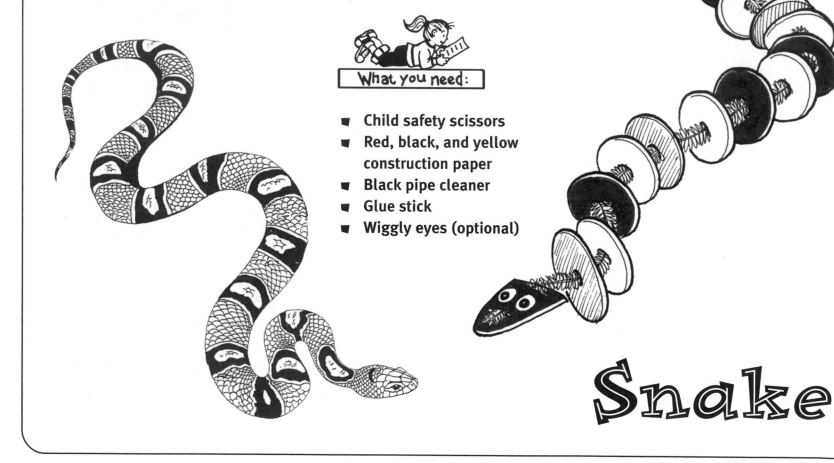

Snake

What you do:

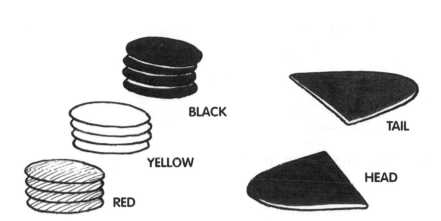

BLACK

YELLOW

RED

TAIL

HEAD

1. Cut out about 20 circles from the red, black, and yellow construction paper. Cut out the snake's head and tail from the black paper.

2. Poke the pipe cleaner through the snake's tail as shown.

Then, thread on alternating colored paper circles for the snake's bands. Leave a space between each circle and continue threading to the end of the pipe cleaner.

3. Thread the snake's head onto the pipe cleaner.

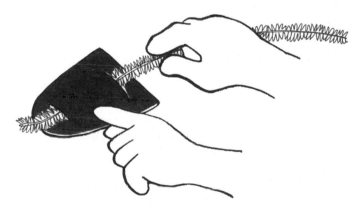

Cut out two small circles of yellow paper for eyes and glue on the head (or glue on the wiggly eyes).

Ask the Zookeeper

Q: *Eeww!* Snakes always look so slimy. Are they yucky to touch?

A: Snakes just *look* slimy because snakeskin is made of solid scales that are very shiny. A snake's skin is really very smooth and dry. Do you think you'd want to feel one to see what it's like?

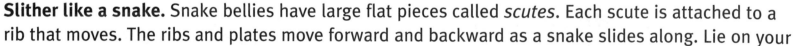

Getting to Know Us

Slither like a snake. Snake bellies have large flat pieces called *scutes*. Each scute is attached to a rib that moves. The ribs and plates move forward and backward as a snake slides along. Lie on your tummy, flat on the ground. Now, try moving forward like a snake. Is it easy or hard?

Play snake in the grass. Mark off an area on a carpeted or wooden floor or on the grass outside. Runners cannot go outside that area, which is called the "snake pit." One player is "it" and crawls around hissing like a snake, trying to touch the other players running in the "snake pit." When a player is tagged, that player is "it."

When my jaws
are open wide,
You'll see my pointy
teeth inside.

Am I a giraffe? An alligator?
A bird?

What you need:

- Child safety scissors
- Green construction paper
- Black and green markers
- Green pipe cleaner

Site: The American alligator lives in the southeastern United States, and the Chinese alligator lives in the Yangtze River region of China.

Alligator

What you do:

1. Cut out an alligator shape from the green paper.

Use the markers to draw the alligator's eyes, mouth, nose, teeth, and scaly skin.

Little Hands Story Corner™

Read *Alligator Tales (And Crocodiles Too!)* by Miles Smeeton.

2. Cut the pipe cleaner in half. Poke each piece through the alligator's body, then bend the pieces for the alligator's feet.

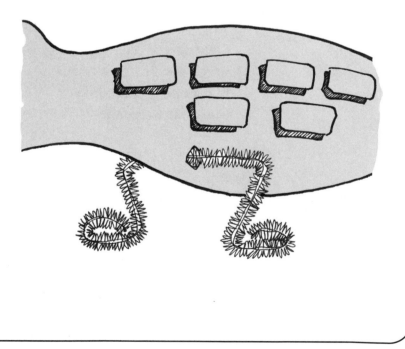

Q: Are alligators and crocodiles the same?

A: No, but people get them mixed up! Crocodiles have narrower, pointed snouts and their lower fourth tooth sticks out when their mouths are closed. Alligator snouts are wider and rounder, and their upper teeth show when their mouths are closed.

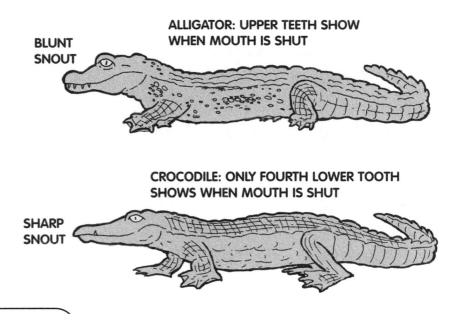

ALLIGATOR: UPPER TEETH SHOW WHEN MOUTH IS SHUT

BLUNT SNOUT

CROCODILE: ONLY FOURTH LOWER TOOTH SHOWS WHEN MOUTH IS SHUT

SHARP SNOUT

Getting to Know Us

Pretend play. Alligators' eyes and nostrils are on top of their heads so they can see and breathe while the rest of their bodies are underwater. Crouch behind a table with just your eyes and nose looking over the table. Pretend to be an alligator. What do you see?

Swim alligator-style. The alligator's long tail moves from side to side, acting like a paddle to move it through the water. Next time you go swimming with a grown-up, paddle your hands or feet side to side. Does paddling water keep you afloat?

I'm a dragon
who doesn't breathe fire.
My scaly skin's
as rough as a tire.

Am I an elephant? A pony?
A Komodo dragon?

What you need:

- Child safety scissors
- Brown paper lunch bag
- Cardboard tube, any size
- Tape
- Scrap of cereal-box cardboard
- Scrap of yellow construction paper
- Tacky glue (available at craft stores)
- Black and brown markers

ENDANGERED

Site: six of the islands of Indonesia in Southeast Asia

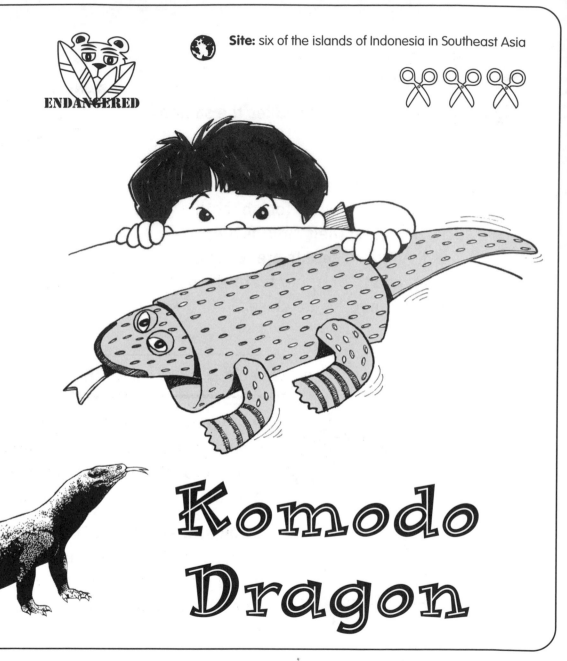

Komodo Dragon

What you do:

1. Cut open the brown paper lunch bag and lay it flat. Wrap the tube in the bag and tape to hold.

2. Cut out the dragon's head, legs, and tail from the scrap cardboard. Cut out a tongue from the yellow paper.

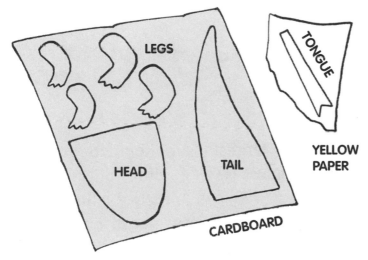

LEGS

HEAD

TAIL

CARDBOARD

TONGUE

YELLOW PAPER

3. Glue the head and tail inside the cardboard tube. Glue on the tongue.

Glue the dragon's legs onto the sides of the tube and allow to dry. Use the markers to draw the eyes, nose, mouth, and scales.

Little Hands Story Corner™

Read *Komodo!* by Peter Sis.

Q: My babysitter read me a story about dragons. Is the Komodo dragon a real dragon?

A: No, those fire-breathing dragons that you read about in your storybooks are not real. They are pretend. The Komodo dragon is actually a very large lizard. It has the word "dragon" in its name because it is so large and scary looking (it looks almost like a dinosaur!).

Getting to Know Us

Leapin' lizards! The Komodo dragon is the world's largest lizard. Komodo dragons can grow to be 10' (3 m) long and weigh up to 310 pounds (140 kg). Some of the world's smallest lizards are the *geckos*. Geckos are only 3" (7.5 cm) long. Use a flexible tape measure and measure something that is 3" (7.5 cm) long. Now measure something that is 10' (3 m) long. That's quite a difference in size!

Learn more. To see a picture of the Komodo dragon, check out the website at <http://www.geocities.com/RainForest/3678/Komodo.html>.

I'm a reptile
crawling on a tree.
Look again;
can you see me?

Am I a raccoon? A chameleon? A frog?

Site: semi-deserts in southern Spain, Africa, the Near East, and western Asia

What you need:

- Sponge
- Black, green, and yellow tempera paints, in dishes or lids
- Small white paper plate
- Child safety scissors
- Scraps of green and red construction paper
- Glue stick
- Tape
- Black marker

Chameleon

What you do:

1. With the sponge, dab the different paints all over the plate to make the chameleon's skin. Allow to dry.

2. Fold the paper plate in half. Cut out the chameleon's head and tail from the green paper and glue them on the inside of the paper plate.

HEAD

TAIL

Tape the plate closed.

3. Cut out a long tongue from the red paper and glue it in the chameleon's mouth.

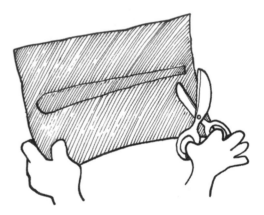

Draw a fly on the tongue. Use the marker to draw the chameleon's legs and eyes.

Little Hands Story Corner™

Read *The Mixed-Up Chameleon* by Eric Carle.

Ask the Zookeeper

Q: Why did we make our chameleons with such long tongues?

A: All chameleons have very long, sticky tongues. They use them to catch their food by quickly flicking them at nearby insects, sort of like licking a Popsicle. Yumm!

Getting to Know Us

The better to see you with! Chameleons' eyes move separately from each other. One eye can look forward while the other looks backward. Look in a mirror and move your eyes from side to side and up and down. Do they move separately or together?

Color me happy. Chameleons can change the color of their skin to express their moods or to match their surroundings to hide from their enemies (that's called camouflage). What color clothing do you like to wear when you're feeling happy? What do you wear when you're feeling sad?

Northern Forest

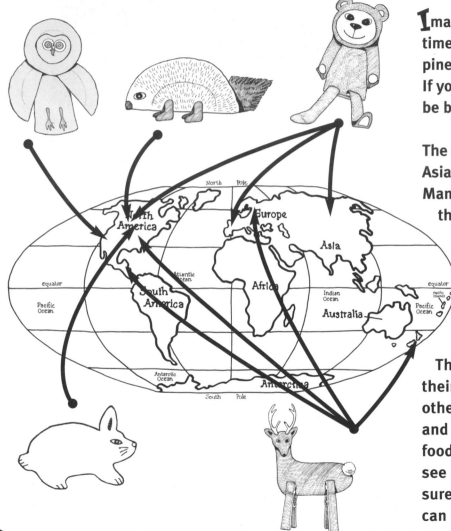

Imagine walking through a northern forest in the summertime. The air feels cool and damp. The thick branches of pine, fir, and spruce trees block out much of the sunlight. If you walked through the same forest in winter, it would be bitterly cold, with deep snow on the ground.

The animals that live in the northern forests of Europe, Asia, and North America are used to the changing seasons. Many of them *hibernate* (kind of like a deep sleep) during the winter or *migrate* (travel) to warmer places to find food. Some animals, like squirrels, store up food during the summer to keep them going through the winter. And some, like the snowshoe hare, have coats that turn white in the winter so they can blend in with the snow and hide from other animals.

The forest is home to many animals. There they find their food, eating leaves, nuts, and berries or hunting other animals. But some woodland animals, like raccoons and deer, have moved into towns and cities, eating the food people have thrown away. Look closely and you may see some woodland animals near your home. But, make sure you never go near one. They may look cute, but they can be very dangerous!

In the winter,
I'm white as snow.
Hippity-hop,
off I go.

Am I a snowshoe hare? A kitten?
An octopus?

Site: the forests of Alaska and northern Canada in North America

What you need:

- Scissors (for grown-up use only)
- Sponge
- Brown and white tempera paints, in dishes or lids
- Brown and white construction paper
- Black, brown, and green markers

Snowshoe Hare

What you do:

1. Ask a grown-up to help you cut the shape of a hare out of the sponge.

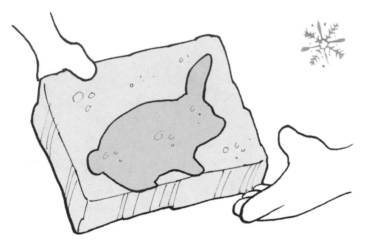

Dab the sponge into the brown paint. Press onto the brown paper for hares.

2. Rinse the sponge clean. Dab the sponge into the white paint. Press onto the white paper.

3. Use the black marker to outline the hares. Use markers to draw a summer scene on the brown paper and a winter scene on the white paper.

Ask the Zookeeper

Q: Why is it called a "snowshoe" hare?

A: Have you ever seen a picture of snowshoes? When you put on a pair, you can walk across the top of the snow without sinking in all the way. The name "snowshoe" hare comes from the hare's huge feet, which have fringes of thick fur. The feet act as snowshoes and prevent the hare from sinking into deep winter snowdrifts.

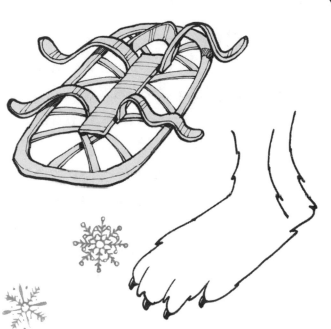

Getting to Know Us

Winter fun! Snowshoe hares live in the forests of Alaska and northern Canada, where winters are long and cold. Draw a picture of the things you like to do when you play in the snow.

Two-toned hares. In the winter, white snowshoe hares blend in with their snowy surroundings. In the summer, their fur turns gray-brown so it blends in with the ground. These changes help them to hide from their enemies. Do you remember the word for this (page 25)? Can you name a reptile that changes color in order to blend in with its surroundings? How about the chameleon (page 97)?

When cold weather comes,
I just can't wait
To crawl in a cave
and hibernate.

Am I a deer? A beaver?
A brown bear?

Site: from Spain across northern Europe through Russia to Japan, and in the northern Rocky Mountains of the United States, Alaska, and Canada

ENDANGERED

What you need:

- Toilet-paper tube
- Brown construction paper
- Tape
- Child safety scissors
- Glue stick
- White construction paper
- Brown marker

Brown Bear

(also known as a grizzly bear in North America)

What you do:

1. Wrap the tube in the brown paper and tape to hold. Cut out the bear's head, arms, and legs from the brown paper. Glue them onto the tube.

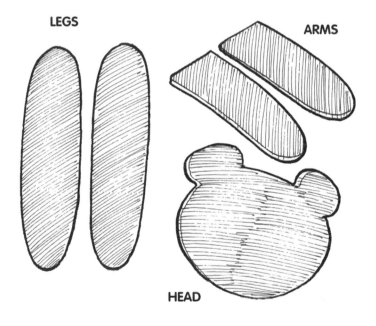

LEGS

ARMS

HEAD

Use the marker to draw ears on the bear's head.

2. Cut out four small circles and one large circle from the white paper.

Use the marker to draw paw pads on the small circles. Glue them onto the arms and legs for the bear's paws.

3. Use the marker to draw the bear's face on the large circle. Glue it onto the bear's head.

Little Hands Story Corner™

Read *Stay Awake, Bear!* by Audrey Wood or "Great Bear," a tale from the Micmac Indians, in *Tales of the Shimmering Sky* by Susan Milord.

Ask the Zookeeper

Q: Do bears really like to give bear hugs?

A: Sometimes it sure looks that way! When two bears fight, they stand up straight on their back legs and grab each other with their arms. It looks as if they're giving each other a big hug, but they're really pushing and shoving each other. Bears are very strong and can be dangerous. So give lots of "bear" hugs, but don't hug a real live bear!

Getting to Know Us

"Bear-ly" walking. Bears walk *pigeon-toed*, with their front feet turned in. That doesn't stop them from being able to run 35 miles (56 km) per hour! (To see how fast that is, ask a grown-up to show you the next time you're riding in the car.) Try bending your knees and walking on your hands and feet. How fast can you go?

This is an animal
you don't want to pet.
Its pointy quills
pose a sharp threat.

Site: North American porcupines are found in the woods from Canada to northern Mexico.

Am I a rhinoceros? A porcupine?
A fox?

What you need:

- Small white paper plate
- Brown and black markers
- Child safety scissors
- Scrap of brown construction paper
- Tape
- Glue stick

Porcupine

What you do:

1. Fold the paper plate in half. Use the markers to draw the porcupine's quills, nose, and eyes.

2. Cut out the porcupine's feet and tail from the brown paper. Tape the tail to the inside of the plate, then tape the plate closed.

Little Hands Story Corner™

Read *Story Time For Little Porcupine* by Joseph Slate.

Glue the feet onto the plate. Use the black marker to draw toes.

Q: My baby brother didn't have any hair when he was born. Does a baby porcupine have quills when it's born, or does it grow them the way my brother grew hair?

A: A baby porcupine is born with long black hair and quills. The quills are soft when the baby is first born, but within hours they harden.

Getting to Know Us

Porcupine treats. Porcupines love the taste of salt! They chew on things they find in country houses, such as leather, canoe paddles, and wooden tool handles. These things probably contain salt from the sweat of the hands that held them. What salty foods do you like to eat? How about potato chips, pretzels, or salted peanuts?

Prickly porcupines! If you see something round and fuzzy up in a tree, it may be a porcupine. Porcupines climb trees to escape their enemies. How do they defend themselves when there are no trees around? They charge backward, and their sharp quills stick into their enemies. Ouch!

I'm a wise old bird.
Can you guess whooo?
At night I hunt for mice;
yes, it's true.

Am I an owl? A robin?
A tiger?

ENDANGERED

What you need:

- Child safety scissors
- 2 white paper plates (1 large, 1 small)
- Brown, orange, and yellow markers
- Brown and black crayons
- Paper fastener*

*Note: Children may put small objects in their mouths. An adult should control the supply of paper fasteners and distribute them as needed.

Spotted Owl

What you do:

1. Cut off the sides of the large paper plate for the owl's wings. The remaining section will be its body.

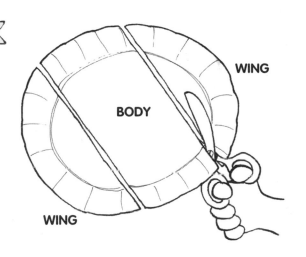

WING

BODY

WING

2. Draw a heart shape in the center of the small paper plate for the owl's face. Use the markers to draw the owl's eyes and beak.

3. Use the paper fastener to attach the owl's wings and head onto the body.

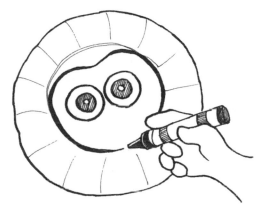

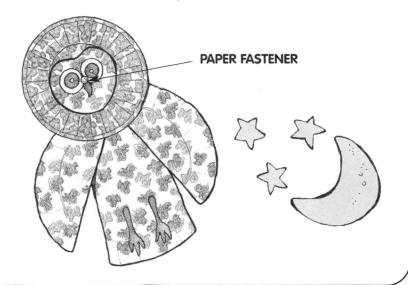

PAPER FASTENER

Use the crayons to color the owl's feathers. Use the brown marker to draw the owl's claws and dark center of the eyes.

Ask the Zookeeper

Q: Why are owls always the wise animals in my storybooks? Are they really wise?

A: Some people think owls *look* wise because of their wide-open eyes that face forward, like human eyes, instead of sideways, like other birds' eyes. Maybe because their eyes are so big, it's easy to think they see everything. What do you think?

Getting to Know Us

Pretend play. All the feathers on an owl, even the stiff wing feathers, have soft edges so that the owl can fly silently. Spread your arms out like wings. Now, silently dip and glide across the room like an owl.

Night sight. Owls have excellent sight. They hunt at night when there is only light from the moon. Their large, round eyes collect as much light as possible. Their sight is so good that they can spot a mouse moving through the grass from high up in the sky. Go outdoors at night. Describe what you see.

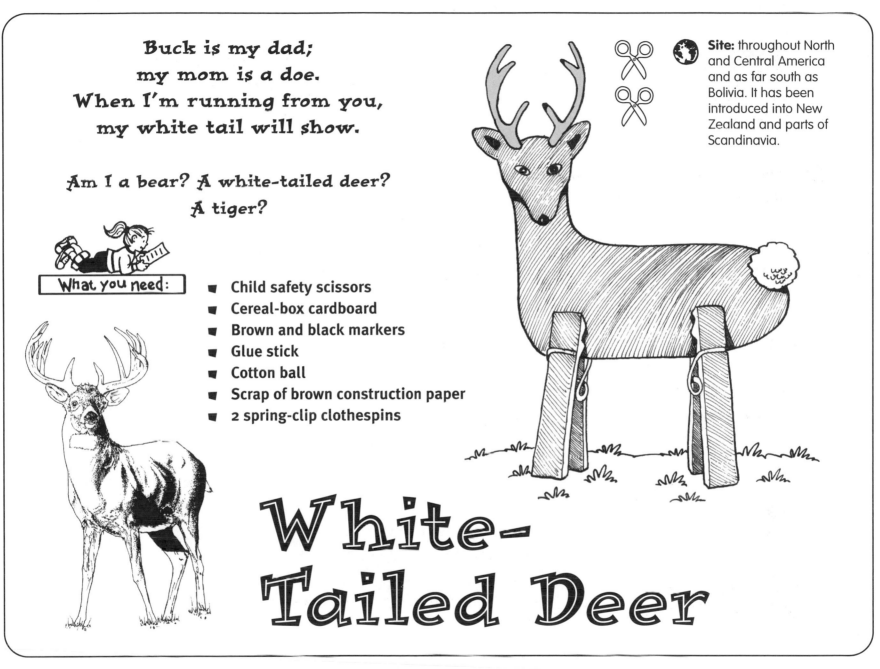

Buck is my dad;
my mom is a doe.
When I'm running from you,
my white tail will show.

Am I a bear? A white-tailed deer?
A tiger?

What you need:

- Child safety scissors
- Cereal-box cardboard
- Brown and black markers
- Glue stick
- Cotton ball
- Scrap of brown construction paper
- 2 spring-clip clothespins

Site: throughout North and Central America and as far south as Bolivia. It has been introduced into New Zealand and parts of Scandinavia.

White-Tailed Deer

What you do:

1. Cut out the shape of a deer's head and body from the cereal-box cardboard.

Use the brown marker to color the deer. Use the black marker to draw the deer's eyes, nose, and ears.

2. Glue on a small piece of cotton for a tail. Cut out the antlers from the brown construction paper and glue onto the head.

3. Use the brown marker to color the clothespins. Clip them to the body to stand the deer upright.

Little Hands Story Corner™

Read Harriet Peck Taylor's *Two Days in May,* an uplifting tale about city folk who save five hungry deer that have wandered into the city.

Q: Some deer in pictures I've seen have antlers, and others don't. Why don't all deer have antlers?

A: It's only the *bucks* (male deer) that have antlers. The bucks use their antlers for fighting and for scraping bushes and trees to mark their *territory* (their area in the forest). If you had antlers, what would you use them for?

Getting to Know Us

Send flag messages. When white-tailed deer feel scared, they wave their large, white tails like a flag. Humans have flag messages, too. For example, waving a white flag means let's not fight, a yellow flag means be careful, a green flag means go, and a red flag means stop or danger. Cut out a flag from colored construction paper, then tape it to a paper-towel tube. Wave your flag to signal to your friends and family.

Baby names. A baby cat is called a *kitten*, a baby bear is a *cub*, a baby camel is a *calf*, and a baby kangaroo is a *joey*. What do you think a baby deer is called? If you guessed a *fawn*, you were correct!

The Big Cats

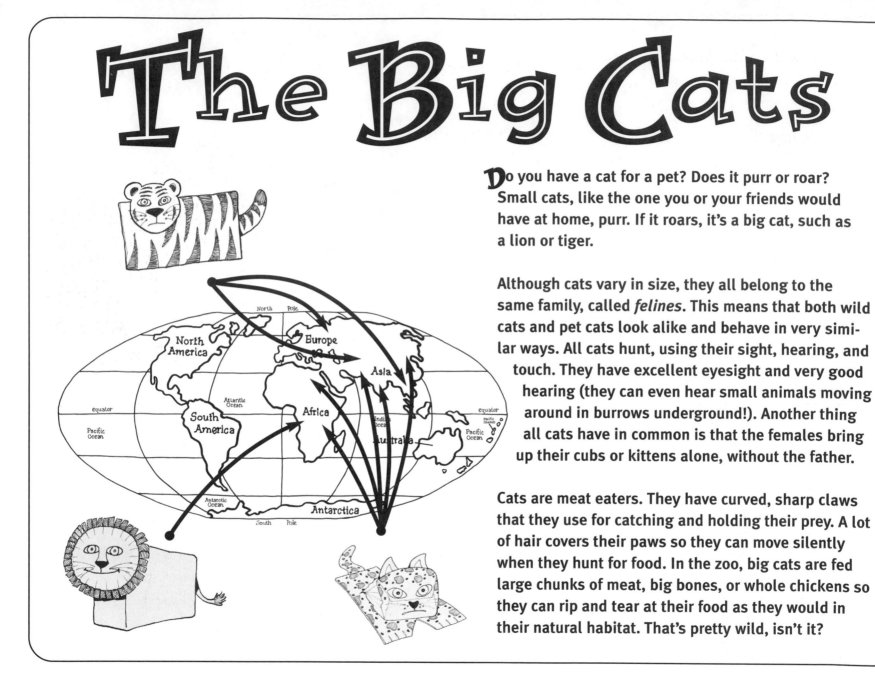

Do you have a cat for a pet? Does it purr or roar? Small cats, like the one you or your friends would have at home, purr. If it roars, it's a big cat, such as a lion or tiger.

Although cats vary in size, they all belong to the same family, called *felines*. This means that both wild cats and pet cats look alike and behave in very similar ways. All cats hunt, using their sight, hearing, and touch. They have excellent eyesight and very good hearing (they can even hear small animals moving around in burrows underground!). Another thing all cats have in common is that the females bring up their cubs or kittens alone, without the father.

Cats are meat eaters. They have curved, sharp claws that they use for catching and holding their prey. A lot of hair covers their paws so they can move silently when they hunt for food. In the zoo, big cats are fed large chunks of meat, big bones, or whole chickens so they can rip and tear at their food as they would in their natural habitat. That's pretty wild, isn't it?

I'm the king
of the African plain.
I roar and toss
my long, flowing mane.

Am I a polar bear? A lion?
A monkey?

Site: Africa, south of the Sahara Desert to South Africa

What you need:

- Cereal box, ¾ oz (21 g)
- Tape
- Child safety scissors
- Brown paper lunch bag
- Glue stick
- Brown and black markers

Lion

1. Open the bottom and side panels of the box so it lies flat. Re-form the box so it is inside out. Tape to hold.

2. Cut off the bottom of the bag. Cut open the paper bag and lay it flat. Wrap the cereal box in the bag and tape to hold.

3. Cut out two circles for the lion's head and a lion tail from the bottom of the bag. Glue the smaller circle onto the bigger circle.

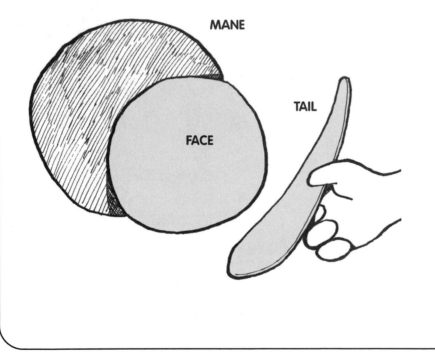

MANE

TAIL

FACE

4. Use the markers to draw the lion's face and mane. Cut fringe for the mane.

Glue the head onto one end of the box. Glue on the tail.

Read *The Lion and the Little Red Bird*
by Elisa Kleven.

Ask the Zookeeper

Q: Why do some lions have manes and others don't?

A: I used to wonder about that, too! The male lion is the one that has a mane. It helps him when he has to fight other lions. What other male animals have you met that look different from their female partners? See page 69 to find out!

Getting to Know Us

Animal groups. Lions are very social. They live and hunt together in family groups called *prides*. Do you have names for groups you belong to? Does your Cub Scout pack have a number? What is the name of your baseball team?

King Leo. The lion is called "the king of the beasts" because of its power and beauty. Do you agree with that name? Can you make up any other names for lions?

When it's hot,
I go for a swim.
With my striped coat on,
I dive right in.

Am I an elephant? A tiger?
A raccoon?

What you need:

- Child safety scissors
- Small white paper plate
- Orange and black markers
- Large white envelope
- Glue stick

Site: from the Russian Far East through parts of China, India, and Southeast Asia

ENDANGERED

Tiger

What you do:

1. Cut out the tiger's head from the center of the paper plate. Cut off a piece of the edge of the plate for the tiger's tail.

2. Use the orange marker to color the front of the envelope, the tiger's head, and the tail. Use the black marker for the tiger's stripes, face, and whiskers.

3. Glue the tiger's tail and head onto the envelope.

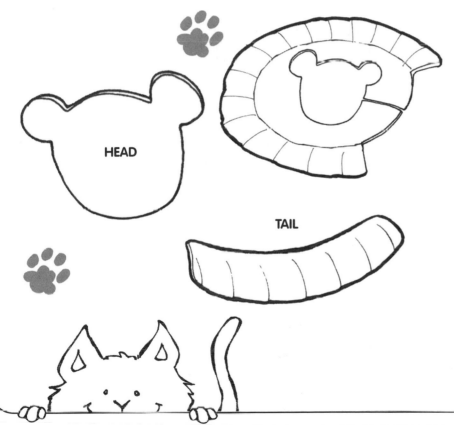

HEAD

TAIL

Little Hands Story Corner™

To learn more about tigers, read *Fast, Strong, and Striped* by Moira Butterfield.

Ask the Zookeeper

Q: Which is bigger, a lion or a tiger?

A: Believe it or not, the tiger is larger and more powerful. The average tiger can be more than 6½ feet (2 m) long and weigh about 500 pounds (225 kg). Wow! So, if a tiger is bigger, why do you think a lion is called the "king of the beasts"?

Getting to Know Us

Balancing act. Tigers use their tails for balance when they run and need to make fast turns. Want to see how it's done? Place a length of string on the ground. Walk along the string, putting one foot in front of the other, like a tightrope walker. Do you use your arms for balance?

Cat Swimmers. Tigers are excellent swimmers. They are one of the few kinds of cats that enjoy being in or near water. What things do you do when you're in the water? Do you swim, bob up and down, or float?

I'm a big cat
up in a tree.
My spotted coat
makes it hard to see me.

Am I a leopard? A duck?
A kitten?

Site: northeastern Africa and nearly all of Africa south of the Sahara Desert, Asia Minor, central Asia and India, China, and Manchuria

What you need:

- 2 brown paper lunch bags
- Old newspaper
- Rubber band
- Child safety scissors
- Scrap of brown construction paper
- Stapler
- Glue stick
- Tape
- Black, brown, and yellow markers

Leopard

What you do:

1. To make the head, stuff the bottom of one bag with a small wad of newspaper. Tightly wrap the rubber band around the neck of the bag.

3. Put the first bag into the second by passing it through the top slit and out the bottom slit.

2. Fold the second bag flat. Cut a V shape into both sides of the top end. Then, cut a horizontal slit one-third of the way down from the top through one side of the bag. Cut a second slit at the bottom edge of the bag.

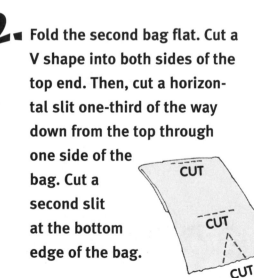

CUT

CUT

CUT

4. Cut out the leopard's tail from the brown paper and insert it into the bottom slit. Staple both pieces in place.

5. Cut out the leopard's ears from the brown paper and glue them onto the bag.

Tape the edges of each V shape together for the leopard's paws. Use the black and brown markers to draw the leopard's eyes, face, whiskers, and spots. Color the eyes yellow.

Little Hands Story Corner™ Read "How the Leopard Got His Spots" from Rudyard Kipling's *Just So Stories.*

Ask the Zookeeper

Q: Why does a leopard have spots?

A: The spots on its coat enable the leopard to blend into wooded grassland as it hunts for its food. That's called camouflage. Remember how the zebra's coat allows it to hide, too (page 25)? How is the zebra's coat different from the leopard's coat? Which one do you like better?

Getting to Know Us

Sitting pretty. Leopards spend a lot of time in trees. Not only do they sleep in trees during the day, but they also eat while sitting in trees. Look up in a tree. What animals do you see there?

Taste test. Leopards curl the tips of their tongues like a spoon to lap up water. They also use their tongues for tasting, scraping meat off a *carcass* (a dead animal), and cleaning themselves. A cat's tongue has a very rough surface. Close your eyes and rub your hand over a sheet of sandpaper to feel a rough texture. That's how a cat's tongue feels!

Activity Index by Skill Level

Check the symbol at the beginning of each activity to quickly assess the challenge level. If a grown-up chooses to prepare some of the pieces of the medium and challenging projects, little hands can join in to color and glue together.

Easy

(for even the littlest hands)

Medium

(requires a few more steps, but with an easy skill level)

Challenging

(more involved projects using fine motor skills)

More Good Books from Williamson Publishing

Other Williamson books by Judy Press!

Over 500,000 sold!
Real Life Award
The Little Hands ART BOOK
Exploring Arts & Crafts with 2- to 6-Year-Olds

AROUND-THE-WORLD ART & ACTIVITIES
Visiting the 7 Continents through Craft Fun

Parents' Choice Approved
**The Little Hands
BIG FUN CRAFT BOOK**
Creative Fun for 2- to 6-Year-Olds

**ARTSTARTS
For Little Hands!**
Fun Discoveries for 3- to 7-Year-Olds

Parent's Guide Children's Media Award
ALPHABET ART
With A to Z Animal Art & Fingerplays

*Early Childhood News Directors' Choice Award
Real Life Award*
VROOM! VROOM!
Making 'dozers, 'copters, trucks & more
A Williamson *Kids Can!*® book for ages 7 to 13

Parents' Choice Honor Award
THE KIDS' NATURAL HISTORY BOOK
Making Dinos, Fossils, Mammoths & More!
A Williamson *Kids Can!*® book for ages 7 to 13

To order, see next page.

The following *Little Hands*® books for ages 2 to 7 are 128 to 160 pages, fully illustrated, trade paper, 10 x 8, $12.95 US.

A *Little Hands*® Read-&-Do book
EASY ART FUN!
Do-It-Yourself Crafts for Beginning Readers
by Jill Frankel Hauser

Parents' Choice Gold Award
FUN WITH MY 5 SENSES
Activities to Build Learning Readiness
by Sarah A. Williamson

FINGERPLAYS & ACTION SONGS
Seasonal Activities & Creative Play for 2- to 6-Year-Olds
by Emily Stetson & Vicky Congdon

Little Hands PAPER PLATE CRAFTS
Creative Art Fun for 3- to 7-Year-Olds
by Laura Check

WOW! I'M READING!
Fun Activities to Make Reading Happen
by Jill Frankel Hauser

The Little Hands PLAYTIME! BOOK
50 Activities to Encourage Cooperation
& Sharing
by Regina Curtis

*Early Childhood News Directors' Choice Award
Parents' Choice Approved
American Institute of Physics Science Writing
Award*
SCIENCE PLAY!
Beginning Discoveries for 2- to 6-Year-Olds
by Jill Frankel Hauser

American Bookseller Pick of the Lists
RAINY DAY PLAY!
Explore, Create, Discover, Pretend
by Nancy Fusco Castaldo

*Early Childhood News Directors' Choice Award
Parents' Choice Approved*
SHAPES, SIZES & MORE SURPRISES!
A Little Hands Early Learning Book
by Mary Tomczyk

Parents' Choice Approved
The Little Hands NATURE BOOK
Earth, Sky, Critters & More
by Nancy Fusco Castaldo

MATH PLAY!
80 Ways to Count & Learn
by Diane McGowan & Mark Schrooten

Prices may be slightly higher when purchased in Canada.